A Life
in Style

A Life
in Style

The autobiography of
car designer Roy Axe

ARPUBLISHING

First published in the United Kingdom in 2010 by
ARPublishing

Copyright © Roy Axe 2010

ISBN 978–0–9566845–0–9

Book production by
The Choir Press

Contents

Acknowledgements

IT WAS A NUMBER OF years ago that I had a call from Keith Adams who was then changing his career course into the world of motor journalism. He had also created an extensive website regarding British Leyland, ARG and the Rover Group, AROnline.co.uk. He asked if I was interested in collaboration on a book about my career. This was to be on a very fast track which proved to be a poor estimate of what was involved.

I had, encouraged by my family, planned some sort of not too technical book of my own to give my family an idea of what my working life was all about. A number of setbacks and delays has made for slow progress but Keith has been an invaluable help in the final preparation of this book. Keith has since progressed in his ambition and is on the staff of one of the most prestigious car magazines, *Octane*.

If I had tried to include the names of all the fine people I have worked with over the years, there would be no room for anything else! Nevertheless so many have helped me over the years and I am very grateful for their support.

I will mention Richard Woolley and David Saddington for their timely help with names and incidents.

Foreword

THIS BOOK IS A COMPILATION of my experiences in the global automotive industry, from 1953 to my retirement in 2000, and is not intended as a complete listing of all the cars I worked on through this period.

For me, these were perhaps the golden years of the industry, and as I write, the automotive business faces its worst crisis since the Great Depression of the pre-war years. The scenario today, however, is very different from the 1930s and I am confident that the industry will survive and perhaps, in the process, shake off its burden of over-capacity that has been a feature of recent times and return to being a strong and profitable business once again.

In this book I make many references to 'Style and Design' and the many battles with engineering. These difficulties were just the teething troubles of changing from an engineering-led industry to one that was more directed to satisfying the customers and their needs.

Design, as a title, does not belong exclusively to any area of creating a car: it is an all-encompassing term for those involved in the creative process.

Styling, however, had the connotation of something superficial and applied, as indeed it was in the early days. When Styling became integrated into the process and took a role at the very beginning of a project, 'Design' became the term used for the function. Engineering is a more technically orientated thing but in no way is one more important than the other.

I say all this to reassure you that I am not anti-engineer in any way, both of these functions work best when they are located together to resolve problems and that is how the business has developed after a great deal of dedication from myself and many others to achieve today's high standards that our customers expect.

Roy Axe, August 2010

Dedication

THIS BOOK IS DEDICATED to my family who have long encouraged me to write an account so they can have a better understanding of what the old man has been doing when away from home so often.

This dedication is first to my wonderful wife, (Pat to my family and Brenda to hers!) We are just a few short months away from our 50th wedding anniversary and she is the love of my life

Then to my dear daughter Jane and her husband George Fenwick who are antique dealers in the lovely village of Broadway, UK.

To their three grown up children, Jenney, Lucy and Charles of whom I am very proud, they are three fine young people.

Then to my son Chris and his wife Rachel. Chris is a chip off the old block as he is a car designer too!

They have five delightful children the eldest being eight. This is our family of young grandchildren, Harry, Katharina (our own drama Queen!), Annika, Carlotta and all new Mieke. They live in Spain where Chris is working but have a home in Germany.

1

The Earliest Years: 1948–1952

IT IS A LUCKY PERSON who becomes aware, at an early point in childhood, of what he or she wants to do in life – and then manages to achieve that goal. I count myself as one of those fortunate people.

I first became aware of cars and trucks in the difficult days of WW2. I lived at that time in a village on the Yorkshire-Lincolnshire border in England in a farming community. My father and his two brothers had inherited various retail businesses and one of these was the local garage business. My Uncle Rupert was in charge there, or at least he was in peacetime but he was away in the Army during the war.

I remember the military vehicles that were around at the time and found them fascinating, particularly things like Bren Gun carriers. There were far more of this type of vehicle around than there were civilian ones as the use of these was severely restricted. But after 1945, things began to change and cars came out of storage and back on the roads.

Most of these cars were basic 1930s transport, such as Austin Sevens and Eights as well as their Morris counterparts. Some were of much earlier vintage; not very exciting today but at the time they were a real status symbol!

There was considerable use of horses in the war, and in this rural area, they were very much more common than cars. I do remember being very impressed when my father had his monthly delivery of flour sacks, which arrived at his warehouse in a Foden, or perhaps it was a Sentinel, steam lorry. In reality, these were little more than a traction engine with a flatbed body, but they were still exciting to me.

The vehicle that made the deliveries had a curved front cab, with the funnel concealed at the back of the cab, and it managed to look quite futuristic. The combination of its striking appearance and the profusion of smoke and noise made this vehicle a formidable and unforgettable sight.

My uncle, freshly de-mobbed at the end of the war, had a black Humber split windscreen Super Snipe, which was a very big and rather swish car at the time.

He used it for a kind of taxi-cum-limousine service, and as he had access to petrol, it was also used for private purposes from time to time. I can well remember watching with envy as my three cousins, Kathleen, Ann and Joan, left to go on holiday, waving as they went from this impressive car.

I remember my uncle had an interesting experience with his Humber. He was out one day, driving on roads bounded by the drainage canals which were a feature of the area, in what seemed like the ever-present fog in the area. He drove under a bridge, which linked two fields, and which was used as a cattle crossing. A cow, rather carelessly, stepped off the bridge and had crash-landed on the Humber.

At least that was my uncle's story, and his insurance claim must have made interesting reading.

An RAF officer who was in the village for a short time had an SS-Jaguar saloon. With its relatively low roof line, this was a most sporting looking car; but the big motoring drama of the time was provided by the three American cars that were around the village from time to time. I still remember them now: a pre-war Packard, which was probably originally a US military VIP vehicle; a Buick sedan with waterfall grille in some rather garish colour; and a step-down Hudson of all things!

The latter two looked as if they had beamed in from another planet. These vehicles appeared in the late 1940s, together with an Austin A40 Devon, which belonged to a commercial traveler who called on my father every two weeks or so. He would take me on part of his tour of business, which was very exciting.

In the war years, we had an airfield built for a training aircrew to fly bombers and if I remember correctly, these were Halifaxes. I became fascinated with aircraft, as I still am today, and as children, my cousins and I would go to the airfield which was about two miles away and stand at the end of the runway as the planes came in. We felt as though we could touch the landing wheels as they flew in, as they seemed so low!

Not many young people today have the chance of that experience!

Sometime around 1949, my parents and I moved to Scarborough in North Yorkshire. There were three major influences with respect to my growing love for things with wheels and wings.

One was that my father was able to arrange an order with the local newsagent to subscribe to *The Autocar, Motor Sport* and an American magazine called *Mechanix Illustrated*. My father had little interest in cars, it was my mother, a farmer's daughter, who was always fascinated by all things mechanical. She had learned to drive when she was nine.

My father was, however, very aware of my enthusiasm and always supported me as my interest developed into a career. The real influence on me, however, was that Scarborough was a centre for car rallies and virtually all those that took place in the north ended in Scarborough.

The Grand Hotel was a very suitable finishing point, and driving tests were held on the Marine Drive and Oliver's Mount racing circuit. Ownership of a modern car in those severely rationed days was confined to the very wealthy and car dealers who seemed to have access to all the exotic cars, and newly introduced models which were normally strictly reserved for the 'Export or Die' programme.

Jaguars, Allards, Jowett Jupiters, Healeys and all manner of other makes, which were usually only able to be seen in books or magazines were there on a regular basis, and this was most inspiring to me. It is difficult to describe the effect that the Jaguar XK120 had on me at that time. Scarborough must have been one of the first places to see one on the road, as Ian Appleyard was a regular competitor in the rallies. His cream XK120 was a real heart-stopper, putting all else in the shade. Of all the wonderful cars of that time the XK120 just stood out as truly exceptional and it still is!

This XK120 was the famous rally car NUB120, driven by Ian Appleyard and his wife Pat (William Lyons' daughter) that still exists today in the Jaguar Heritage museum. I have a recollection that the first car was NUB 120, but maybe my memory is playing tricks!

Another thing that influenced me was the aforementioned Oliver's Mount, which was the venue for major motorcycle races, with all the big names of the day, and the very latest bikes. I cannot say that I have ever been interested in riding motorcycles but I love the look of them, even today.

What a feast for the senses all this was to a young boy with a growing passion for these forms of transportation. I carefully read my magazines, and became familiar with the technical terms of the business with a growing awareness that I had a great interest in the way cars looked. From the American magazine, and from brochures that I sent away to the American motor companies for (they all replied and sent lots of material back to me), I became aware that there were places where people designed the shapes that I was so interested in.

My friend Steve Williamson and I would walk for miles around the Marine Drive and sea front in Scarborough, talking about all this, and many other things too. Steve was not as interested in cars as me, but he was very encouraging. I eventually became a car designer, and he became a QC, and we are still firm friends today.

2

Pursuing an Ambition: 1953–1959

THE TIME WAS APPROACHING when I would leave the Scarborough Boys' High School, and I had only one real ambition in mind but how to achieve it? My teachers were scornful of such an ambition, suggesting instead that being a doctor or lawyer would be a better way to go. My family also had no idea what was needed to become a car designer.

Another uncle suggested that if I wanted to design cars, I should perhaps join a car company. Well, this sounded like a remarkably good suggestion! I had always liked Rootes' cars, and so we wrote to them. My father took me down to Coventry for an interview, where I was told again that I didn't really want to design (style) cars at all! It would be better for me to do an engineering apprenticeship, I was told. This could be in body engineering, if it really must be!

And that is what I did. But with a determination that when an opportunity arose, as I felt sure it would, I would be able to become a car stylist.

As an apprentice at Rootes, I had an excellent grounding in body engineering. The draughtsmen there spent a great deal of time explaining things and giving me an understanding of the engineering side of car body design that would stand me in very good stead later on. I also spent time in the experimental shop, and on the MIRA test track in Nuneaton, where it was always exciting to see other products, particularly Jaguars, roaring round the high speed circuit.

I spent time on the assembly track, too. I remember working on the Humber Hawk line fitting dash panels into the bodies on the line. The procedure was to set up a crude wooden bench where the front seats would eventually be. Sitting on this bench, two of us would have the whole dash assembly passed in to us. We would then locate it by banging it into place between the windscreen pillars with our feet and then driving a few metal screws in to hold it.

All this was a mile away from the precision of today and does explain why cars in those days lacked a little refinement of build quality!

About half way through my training, I was placed in the pattern shop at the Ryton plant. Things were very quiet there at the time, and I was allowed to sit in a corner drawing cars, my favourite occupation. The foreman in charge was called Cecil, and he was very interested in what I did. In conversations he learned about my ambition to become a car stylist and he became determined to help.

Luckily for me, he had some connections over at Humber Road, and sent my sketchbooks to Ted White, the head of the Styling office there. As a result, I was contacted and told that I could go over to the styling department the next Monday for three weeks as a sort of trial, I guess. They had never done anything like this before so talk about being in the right place at the right time!

I had a great deal to thank Cecil for and it was a great opportunity. I duly arrived in the studios on the designated day and I never left, except to do my National Service in the army. The people in the studios at Rootes at that time were very influential on my career. They were, in fact, my mentors. If I had not had their guidance and help I undoubtedly would not be where I am today.

On my arrival in the studios, I was introduced to the team of around six people. At that time Engineering was very dominant and in control, with the styling department reporting to the Chief Body Engineer.

Stylists in the studio at that time were, in the main, art school trained, with two exceptions: Ted White, Head of Styling at that time, and Ted Green, his assistant. The two Teds had been together at British Light Steel Pressings (BLSP) in London, a Rootes owned company. They were responsible for the Sunbeam-Talbots.

The styling studio, in the late 1940s and early '50s was at Humber Road Coventry, and the chief there at that time was Peter Wilkes and his assistant, Peter Ashmore. Long before I arrived, the two Peters had left after some sort of dispute. I am not sure what this was, but it could well have been the relationship that William Rootes had with the American industrial designer, Raymond Loewy, had put noses out of joint!

To replace these two was difficult, and obviously someone who was not going to get upset by any other arrangements would be a desirable choice. The two Teds had also appeared to have been in difficulties, but I am not sure why.

They had been responsible for the design of the new Sunbeam-Talbot 80 and 90 models. The design of these cars, which went on to be successful international rally stars, was very nice. I have seen references to suggest that the design should be credited to Loewy, but Ted White said otherwise and this is confirmed in an article I have about Tucker Madawick, Loewy's man in London at that time.

He says that the 'Two Teds' designed the exterior, but it was the interior that was done by Loewy. Ted White explained to me that the roof of the 90 was carried over from the earlier Sunbeam model, which was quite an accomplishment in itself, and that the drop tanks fitted to late WW2 jet fighter planes had inspired the front wing shape. This is all very plausible.

Their excellent work on the Sunbeams showed a talent for design, and these two men were engineers, so would not object to working for an engineer. The new studio set up put them in as a section of Body Engineering headed by George Payne who, of course, they knew well. They were also 'on trial' so to speak!

Ted White was a quiet man, but as I found out much later, someone with a good sense of

The Rootes Experimental Shop during the late '40s was a fertile learning experience for an ambitious young designer.

humour. Ted Green was almost reclusive, having responsibility for the big Humbers, which only he was allowed to work on.

Tucker Madawick also claims the work for the new post-war Humber Hawk exterior, which in its earliest form resembled the Hillman Minx Loewy design. The rest of the staff was from an art school background. Some good people, such as Brian Powell, Hume Cook and Ron Bradshaw, had already left by then and gone to Ford.

The designers there included the very capable Geoff Crompton, who came from Lancashire and who taught me a great deal. His wife Pauline was also a member of the team, as the colour and trim stylist. She was also very dedicated and went on to hold the same sort of position at Ford. Then there was Ron Wisdom, who was one of the real characters of the place and who was capable of some very fine design ideas but was something of a loner.

He was a good friend of the Cromptons, and became a good friend of mine, too, for many years. In addition, there was also a man called Howard Beasley, who was something of a renegade; he seemed to do more of the modelling work than sketching, although I have seen him do quite a few wild sketches too but he was definitely a renegade, and Ted White saw him as an enemy in the camp, and quite a disruptive one.

These people with their art school backgrounds were as alike as chalk and cheese compared with the 'Two Teds'. As a result, there were two camps, and neither had a lot of respect for the other.

There was a difference even in the look of the two groups. The 'Two Teds' were conventionally dressed in dark suits, whereas the others were in full art school regalia which at the time was a combination of sport jackets, 'drainpipe' trousers and 'brothel creeper' shoes! They looked quite spectacular walking down the main drive of the Humber road plant in the early 1950s with the engineers in the building to the left and a machine shop to the right.

I will leave it to your imagination to picture the scene and the comments!

I was taken under the wing of the stylists, and was taught all they knew. I must have done well from the word go, as I was never under pressure to leave and I completed my training there without question. Everything was done the hard way, though designs were sketched to scale, which was demanded by Sir William Rootes, as he was known by then.

The sketching techniques were of their time, using primitive materials. Nothing sophisticated was available until much later on, when there was Ford, and later, Chrysler influence.

There was a real fear that if left to our own devices, we would exaggerate the lines, and the final car in 3D would not be what was required. Decisions were made from the sketches, and quarter scale Plasticine models were then made. After modifications, the stylists translated them into full size drawings.

After that, templates were taken from the model, and a full-size drawing made in some detail with some surface development on it in key areas. This layout was then taken to the woodworkers downstairs and made into full-size model cars with full interior made from wood. They were works of art! The seats and doors were trimmed out so that the mock-ups could be sat in and evaluated.

'Management' – which really meant Sir William – then made modifications and changes were made by spoke-shaving the wood into the new shape as he directed. Or by gluing wood strips on, as required, and then smoothing it to the new shape until the model was finally approved. At this point, the finished model was repainted, and was effectively indistinguishable from a real car.

All the instruments had to be lettered up by hand (no Letraset in those days) and all the parts, such as the hand-brake handle, mocked up separately. All this was accomplished by the handful of stylists alongside the wood shop workers. This was my training ground, and it gave me the chance to do a bit of everything.

Going back to Peter Wilkes and Peter Ashmore, they did something which had an influence on me, even before I went to Rootes.

They made a car model that was exhibited in the Transport section of the 1951 Festival of Britain to illustrate the possible future of car design. I visited the Festival of Britain, as part of a school party, which was quite an adventure in itself.

In the Transport Pavilion I came across this model car, which was, as I recall, something around one third scale. It was a 'see through' design and a forward control layout with the bonnet at the rear, with the driver and front passenger sitting over the front axle line.

In fact the design layout of that car was followed a few years later by some of the Italian designers. I remember Ghia doing a similar thing, and Pininfarina had a rather wilder example with a kind of X-formation of the road wheels, front and rear wheels being on centre line, with the middle two being outboard. It was quite a forward-looking thing, from an exciting period of design. It came at the time when Raymond Loewy was brought-in to Rootes.

Loewy was employed by William Rootes back in 1939, but because of the war there was no time for him to do anything. But no doubt there was time to think about what was going to happen afterwards and he returned soon after the end of the war.

Loewy was a very influential designer in the USA, and he was really in the vanguard of what was known as Industrial Design. It is interesting that many of the designers in the studio when I arrived at Rootes described themselves as industrial designers (rather than stylists, and certainly not engineers).

Before the war, Loewy had done some iconic design pieces, one of the most famous being the torpedo shaped Pennsylvania locomotive. This was a steam engine, a kind of US equivalent of the Nigel Gresley streamliners, which had appeared in the UK in the late 1930s.

After the war he came very much into prominence in the car industry by designing the 1953 Studebaker Starlight and Starliner. These two cars were quite a breath of fresh air in the USA. This was a time when American cars were very clumsy, loaded with chrome, and going in a direction that was hard for Europeans to take.

Along came the Studebaker Starlight, a very svelte smooth car with minimal decoration, and was very effective in the market place in terms of people's reactions. Unfortunately, for US buyers weaned on cars with heavy chrome, it wasn't the commercial success Studebaker hoped it would be. In fact, in the later years, it also became too laden with chrome, and was positively ugly in its final iterations.

Following on from the Starlight in 1962–63, was Loewy's Avanti, which was probably an even more advanced vehicle for its day and unlike anything else on the American market. It was one of the first cars to have a Coke bottle shape. By that I mean, if you look at a car in plan view, most cars have slightly convex shaped sides when viewed from above.

The difference with the Avanti, is that it was 'nipped in' about the area of the rear doors and then bulged out again over the rear wheels. Viewed from the side, the same effect was achieved by dropping the belt line just before the rear wheels then rising over them so the visual effect was a kind of nipping in of the centre part of the car towards the rear wheel area. As Coke bottles had a similar shape, this is where the nickname came from.

In fact, it was probably more influenced by what was known as the area rule for fuselage shapes of the advanced fighter planes. In order to achieve high aerodynamic efficiency, there was a relationship between the cross section of the fuselage, including the wings.

Where the wings started to sprout from the fuselage the cross section was kept constant and the fuselage was nipped-in in the area of the wings to keep this consistency. If you look at some of the early fighters you will see that Coke bottle shape rather distinctly when viewed from above.

The Loewy presence at Rootes in the late '40s and early '50s was by two or three of his designers, not Raymond himself. They were involved in the design of the first full-width Hillman Minx in 1948, and later the rather strangely named (to our ears today) 'Gay Look' Hillman and Sunbeam models!

This was essentially before my time, but these models set the style for Rootes.

Ken Howes joined the styling office, again with some connections from the Rootes family. Ken had been with Raymond Loewy in the USA, so perhaps that's where the connection was. He was always very friendly to me, although he could be very stand-offish, and in later years he became quite a recluse. He carried something of a chip on his shoulder regarding the fact that he never got any recognition, in his opinion, for the Sunbeam Alpine, the late '50s second version, that is.

Ken had also been at Ford in the USA, although he was English born (I think he came from Swindon).

A very small team was created: Ken, Geoff Crompton and myself, with me being very much the 'gofer', the learner, on the project. But it was very good experience for me. Ken was not responsible to Ted White, but had a direct line into the Rootes family.

The Alpine was made as a scale model, which Ken and Geoff worked on, for a period of time. In its earliest days, the model had a large arrowhead shaped scallop in the side, which came right up to just behind the front wheels, and which went right to the back of the fins.

This stayed with the model for a long time and it was only in the final iteration, just before the car came out, that it was filled in. I can't remember why, but it may have been something to do with manufacturing but I have to say that the model looked much better without it!

A full-size wooden model was made which was approved for production on a platform chassis that was derived from a Hillman Husky. This was a very nice design and I was very lucky to have been involved in it and widening my experience with two designers who were willing to help me along.

There was another man there, called Vister De Wit, a South African. He was there because he had a friend in the Rootes family who he was able to contact and get this job while his wife was studying at the Royal College of Music in London.

He was quite a big guy, notable for sitting around in his large black overcoat even in the warmest days of summer, and for smoking a positively huge pipe which he spent most of the time filling with tobacco and only occasionally lighting. When he did light it, it took a long time to get this tobacco underway and therefore a lot of matches were thrown away in the process.

Vister was a prodigious producer of sketches, he turned them out at a fantastic rate; they were usually pretty wild stuff, and I should say about 90 per cent were screwed up and thrown over his shoulder. Behind him the growing pile of screwed up paper combined with the lighted matches from his pipe made it invariable that a fire would break out, and there was panic when it happened, and we all scrambled to put it out. He would do that over and over again.

I remember going to the cinema with him once. It was summer, and we sat there in the dark, warm cinema, with Vister in his big black overcoat, completely blocking the view of people behind. Then right in the middle of the show, he lit his pipe and which caused *huge* clouds of smoke to circulate through the cinema. He really was a larger-than-life character.

There were many other stories regarding Vister and his wild behaviour. He was an interesting guy. He was working with a South African company to produce a body design for a small sports car designed by Bob Van Niekerk, which became the GSM Delta Dart. The car was produced and it really was quite nice. The body mouldings were used for other cars too.

Another story I remember about him was going down to London with Geoff Crompton and his wife to see a play by Sam Wanamaker, *The Iceman Cometh*. We went to call in on Vister at his flat, and were all taken aback to be received by Vister and his wife sitting up in bed! The whole visit had them remaining in bed! Such was the eccentricity of Vister De Wit. Vister eventually returned to South Africa and we really heard no more about him after that.

Later on in the 1950s Bill, later known as William, Towns joined the studio in a similar sort of situation to myself as a trainee at Rootes.

It was a sort of confirmation that taking me in to train internally had worked and could be repeated.

Bill and I shared desks, side by side, for some time and we even shared a flat with others for a short period. Rex Fleming also joined, as a clay modeller initially, but became a stylist later on. Rex was someone who I had a long-term working relationship with, as I will write about later.

Another person who joined at that time was Barry Ecclestone. He was a Birmingham art school trained industrial designer when he joined us. He was a very keen automotive man and quite a character too. I still correspond with Barry to this day. He and I shared a flat for a period of time and I developed a great deal of respect for him and a good friendship. These then are the people that taught me my business, sketching, modelling, and so on.

Events unrelated to styling during this period that are worth recording here concern a friend of mine, David Gibson, who was also a Pupil trainee at Rootes Motors in the 1950s, and he was ahead of me by perhaps three years.

David and I both lived in Scarborough at the time, or rather my parents and David's mother did, and David's girlfriend Janet (who became his wife) was there too. David had arranged with the local dealer, Arundale's of Scarborough, to deliver new cars up there at the weekends.

David had to go away on an assignment for a while and I took over. When he returned, the two of us shared this arrangement by David driving his car up to Scarborough and me taking the new one, with the pair of us returning in David's car. When David did not have his car available, we both went up in the new car together and came back on the train.

David was a good friend, and a vigorous driver, and I am pleased to say that I am still in touch with him. The story relates to an MG PB Airline that David owned; this was a pretty, pre-war car in light and dark blue. David's car was Ford-engined and was definitely in a somewhat dilapidated condition, with various loose joints and other issues, and it was not too precise on the road but money was tight.

On this particular occasion we drove briskly together, up North, and not having a new car that weekend we drove in David's car there and back. On the way up in the dark, the car started weaving around quite badly, which in itself was not an unusual situation, but this got out of hand to the point where it was weaving right across the road. Things were getting rather dangerous. Somewhere around Ollerton, in the dark, we came down a hill to a roundabout, and there was a garage to the side, which was open.

We drove in and parked the car, and the owner, a rather portly gentleman in oily blue overalls, came out and asked us what was wrong.

We said, 'Well, we have driven this car for some distance, and it's getting pretty wild in terms of its handling, wandering about on the road.' We proceeded to go into a long explanation as to what it might be: track rod ends, half shafts, all kinds of reasons why this might happen, and being engineering students at the time, we of course knew all these things!

Our host listened rather stoically, and in the end said that he needed to get the car on the ramp for a closer look, which he duly did. We waited for him to reappear, and when he did, we launched into another tirade as to what these problems might be and again, the garage owner listened very stoically.

After all this he finally said, 'Well lads, it could be the half shafts, it could be your track rod ends, and it could have been any one of many other things you talked about but personally I'd go for the puncture in your nearside rear tyre!'

Now that was a remark to make two engineering students feel very small indeed . . .

The next incident was with David and I driving together to Scarborough, and this time in a Hillman of some kind, perhaps a van. We were driving somewhere north of Goole going the back way to Scarborough when with a big clang, the linkage to the handbrake fell off. But we thought we could proceed without the handbrake, it's not too much of a problem. We continued, but a little further on, there was an almighty noise from the back, and there had been some catastrophic occurrence in the rear brake drum, which had resulted in severing the brake fluid pipe.

So we had a car with no brakes whatsoever in Yorkshire, in the dark, in the cold, in the winter time, and we were effectively stuck. We decided to proceed by slowing the car right down through the gears, and when we got to a halt sign, we held the car back by the passenger jumping out and effectively holding the car to a standstill.

There was not much traffic around in those days and it was very quiet on those back roads at night and in the dark. We did find a garage, but there was nothing we could do other than hammer over the brake lines, which the garage owner helped with. He then filled up the reservoir but we still had effectively no brakes at all but we proceeded carefully to Scarborough, which was still another 50 miles away.

We elected not to go down the very steep Staxton Hill for obvious reasons, and did a detour around Bridlington, but we got ourselves all the way to Scarborough like that, and somehow I don't think we could have done that in this day and age.

Back at work and a short time before I left to go into my National Service, something happened which actually caused quite a revolution in the styling studios at Rootes: Bob Saward and Tom Firth joined from Ford. That company had its design studios established for some considerable period of time in the UK, and was very heavily influenced by the USA operation.

There were some quite well known characters down there, one of them being Colin Neal, an English designer, whose elder brother Eric Neal was a friend of mine and who was responsible for the Jensen 541. Colin was to figure quite significantly in my future as well.

What Bob Saward and Tom Firth brought from Ford was, first of all, some much more sophisticated sketching techniques that were in use by Ford at the time. Most of the sketch work was done by crayon, on rough art paper, and often, coloured paper.

Bob and Tom had some good advanced techniques, which we all quickly embraced, and which improved our sketch techniques considerably.

Then the other, perhaps more significant thing they did, was to introduce clay modelling as distinct from Plasticine modelling into the styling studios at Rootes. This was really a major move because it was the death knell for the wooden models, which were built downstairs in the wood shop.

All the wood shop had left to do once clay modelling was introduced was to build the bucks, or armatures as they were known, to which the clay was applied and a model was suitably shaped in full size as well as still doing them in scale form.

This was a major change, and to do it a man called Fred Barrett was brought in from Ford. Fred was a modeller and took charge of the new modelling operations. Fred and I later had a working relationship lasting quite a long time.

That is the background of those people who I worked with and taught me my business. It was from that knowledge base that, when I eventually came out of my National Service in 1961, I was ready to move ahead into greater things.

3

An Interlude: 1959–1961

IHAD BEEN GRANTED A delayed date for my National Service, but on completion of my training at Rootes, I was called in. National Service ended soon after I was called up, but I had to complete the required two years anyway. Nothing of particular interest occurred in my service over this period as the system wound down but it was a period of time when events of a life-changing kind took place.

From my camp near London, I went up to town one evening to meet my cousin Jean who was a Ward Sister in the London Hospital. With her was her friend Pat, who was Theatre Sister at the Mildmay Mission hospital in the East End. Pat had trained with Jean and they were close friends. This meeting blossomed into a romantic relationship, which in turn led to marriage. It was something of a whirlwind courtship involving trips to Yorkshire and to Exeter, where Pat's parents lived.

My parents had given me one of the newly introduced Minis. These were still an unusual sight at that time, and they did not prove too popular at first. There was a little confusion also with regard to the name of my young lady, as her family always referred to her by her first Christian name Brenda.

Pat came into use in her hospital time as they had too many trainee nurses called Brenda! To this day, my side of the family and all friends call her Pat, while her side of the family calls her Brenda!

The Mini had a hectic life, and there were many incidents. I learned to remove the cylinder head and re-grind valves by the roadside, as they frequently burned out. This procedure became part of a glorified pitstop, and was completed in ever-shorter times.

About a week before we were married, I travelled down to Exeter, where the ceremony was to be held. Pat had gone there in the lead up to the wedding. I needed to return to camp for a few days, and then planned to return to Devon a day before the big event.

Travelling towards London on that gloomy wet night, I came around a bend at a reasonably brisk pace, only to encounter a stream of mud right across the apex. The Mini skidded as I lost control, and spun off backwards, down a slope, turning over sideways and end-on-end to come to rest on its side under a barbed wire fence. It was an unforgettable crash.

The Mini had managed to miss all the trees on the way down, but I could not open the door as the barbed wire held it shut. I managed to crawl out of the sliding side window (I was a little slimmer in those days) completely unharmed (there were no seatbelts then). As I walked back up the slope, I came across a few chaps who seemed to be searching for something. They had seen my car come off the road and were 'looking for the driver'.

Establishing, to their surprise, that I was the driver, and that they were also doing National Service, they quickly released the Mini and we all carried it back to the road.

There were numerous dents, and what later turned out to be a bent wheel, but otherwise all was okay, and I drove on back to camp without further incident. A few days later I returned to Exeter, the wedding went well, and we left for our short honeymoon in the battered Mini!

The car finally completed 90,000 hard miles in around two and a half years.

For a time we stayed with my cousin Kathleen and her husband Ray at Havant Island near Portsmouth, which was near to where I was stationed. Ray was, and still is, a keen vintage racer, and at that time had a very nice Lagonda 2 Litre. Havant was very close to Goodwood, and so we had an excellent summer visiting the track. The highlight was spectating at the wonderful RAC Tourist Trophy race in 1960, which was won by Stirling Moss in the beautiful Rob Walker Ferrari 250SWB.

I completed my service and returned to the Rootes styling department late in the winter of 1961. Our daughter Victoria (known by her second Christian name, Jane, just to keep up the names confusion!) was born on Christmas Day of that year in Scarborough.

Pat had been a midwife and was determined to have her Christmas lunch at home at my parents' house. Late in the afternoon, she announced that we had better get to the hospital, and quickly. I drove the Mini briskly down to the hospital and just in time, too. Jane was born shortly after.

Still, the upheaval on Christmas Day was worth it – we were given a free cot by a local store for a Christmas baby!

I was a very different man when I returned to Rootes. I now had a wife and new family. This caused me to take a more serious view of a future career in design.

Rootes to Chrysler: 1961–1967

WHEN I RETURNED, THE cast of characters had not changed much. The Cromptons had left, and Rex Fleming had risen in the ranks and was now a stylist on the main project at the time, the Swallow. Soon afterwards, Tom Firth returned to Ford, and new people continued to arrive. The Super Minx was in the final design stages, as was the Imp, and I only did minor work on these projects.

Project Swallow, which was led by Rex Fleming, was something quite bizarre. A new engineering director, Peter Ware, came on board to replace Bernard Winter, and brought David Hodkin with him.

David had been involved in the ERA D-type, a post-war single-seat racing car, which Stirling Moss had been driving without much success. David's background was in racing cars, and he was a nice chap, but perhaps not too well suited to the cost sensitive world of production cars. Given that the Swallow project was designed to replace the bread-winning Minx range, this was probably not the best appointment for him.

There had already been problems replacing the Minx, and we had been left with something rather bigger, the Super Minx. Because it was so much larger, it became an additional model line, as it was too expensive to replace the smaller car. This was a complexity that the company really did not need.

The Rootes studio group.

The Swallow intended to replace the Minx, but was a very different animal. It had a transverse, aluminium six-cylinder engine, mounted at the rear. The radiator was in the front – a plumbing nightmare – and all in all it was far too complex and costly to sell as a simple four-door family car. Especially one planned to sell at Hillman Minx type prices below the Super Minx range!

Lord Rootes had retired at this point, and the other Rootes family members were running the company. They were being presented with a lot of data on the Swallow at different times and not all was good reading. For example, there would be a chassis layout and costs presentation, and then later, another presentation would be for the body.

Then the ancillaries and components costings were moved from one category to another to make the project appear less expensive than it actually was. This was a practice familiar now to followers of the political scene today but was a dangerous sleight of hand when applied to an industrial project!

Because of this project mismanagement there was considerable confusion as to what the total cost of the car would be. Because the car was presented in this fragmented manner, the Rootes family were led into believing that it was hitting its cost targets, when in truth it had no chance whatsoever.

It was a complex and very advanced car, and it certainly didn't have a mass-market specification. There were other bizarre difficulties as well, such as how to make an estate car version, very difficult with a transverse engine stuck across the rear wheels just where you wanted to have the load compartment!

Somebody once had the bright idea of saying all we had to do was put a table on the top of the engine, and that would be a useful feature and this idea was actually mocked up. The whole thing was just crazy.

I remember being in the drawing office, which was upstairs from the experimental department, when one of, if not the only, prototype was wheeled out into the driveway. We were looking out of the window down at this thing, when out it came and they started it up – there was a kind of a bang, and a huge cloud of steam completely enveloped the car. It disappeared, there were lots of giggles and smirks, and the prototype was quickly pushed back into the experimental department and disappeared for further work!

What had happened was that the water hoses had burst. I can't remember how many feet of hose there was, but it was an enormous amount.

Soon after that Lord Rootes, as Sir William had become, was brought into a meeting, where I was in attendance for some reason. The project was presented to Lord Rootes in the same fragmented way but he saw through that immediately.

He could obviously see very clearly that there was something radically wrong. Eventually these costs were brought together in front of him and he absolutely went wild. He got so furious about the whole thing that he fired David Hodkin on the spot. The rest of the Rootes family was suitably chagrined, I am sure, but they had to go along with his Lordship at the time and that was the end of the Swallow.

The design team had been doing this work, as a special group located in the engineering office. They had taken Rex Fleming out of the styling department and put him on his own with the engineering team to style the Swallow.

No one else in styling really had a go at this project, but when it was cancelled there was a complete about-turn relating what car could replace the Minx. This is how the Arrow, or the 'A' car as it was known, came about.

Harry Sheron led the A Car project team. This led to the emergence of Harry Sheron into a senior engineering position. He was a no-nonsense down-to-earth sort of guy, and fully understood the concept of cost containment, and was all gung-ho and ready to run this project. Rex was the lead designer, but we all had a go at the style of the car.

The benchmark was the first generation Ford Cortina, a roaring success in the marketplace at the time. It was just so right, simple and stylish. I was so impressed by it, that I bought a new Cortina GT myself. This was a car I ran for a while, a red one with a black interior. It was great, went well, and was a very nice car, but it was the only Ford I have ever owned. The Lotus Cortina went a stage even further than the GT, of course, and was a very successful saloon racecar.

The Arrow was inspired by the Cortina's simplicity. It was a car designed to be produced very simply, at a very low cost, to sell for a low price; and the end result was really a masterpiece in its day in terms of its simplicity, ease of manufacture and fitness for purpose. The look was very European, which added to its appeal. Rootes believed it should make a vehicle of this kind, the complete antithesis of the Swallow.

That was the brief that Harry Sheron and others had, to produce a car with that kind of simplicity and ruggedness and market appeal.

Peter Ware brought in a new chief of the experimental department, a guy called Peter Wilson. He died just a few years ago, and he was quite a character. He had been in the fleet air arm, where his connection with Peter Ware had taken place, and he was a carrier

Project Arrow development images

In 1963, the Arrow proposals had a distinct look of the Imp about them.

By the following year, these had been developed into full-sized clay models.

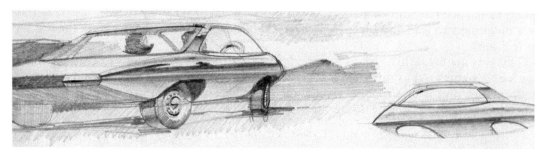

While the simple Arrow was being styled, Roy Axe worked on a number of more exotic ideas.

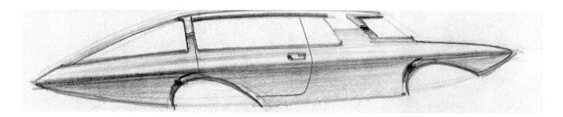

pilot. He had been a Bristol Cars works Le Mans driver, and he was excellent behind the wheel. I did get to know Peter well much later on, and he became, I felt, a rather lonely character in the end before he died.

We all had an opportunity to produce quarter scale models, and eventually it was Rex's design that was chosen based on his work on the Swallow (but with a grille added at the front). It was made into a full-size model, which was tweaked a little bit here and there as time went along, but essentially the quarter scale model became the actual car. It was a fairly smooth process, because of the need to do this thing as fast as possible due to all the time that had been lost doing the Swallow.

But this was the Peter Ware engineering group that had formed at the time and in some way Tim Fry was tied into that. Tim recently died too, and I never really knew exactly what these connections were. I had been told that there were some family ties between Peter Ware and Tim, but I don't know if that's true.

Michael Parks, who later gained considerable fame as a Ferrari engineer and racing driver, together with Tim Fry, had been responsible for the initial design and development of the Hillman Imp. The car was later styled very competently by Bob Saward, but as the programme wound down, Tim was moved into the styling department but was not responsible to Ted White. He did work on the fins on the back of the early Rapier. Lord Rootes came back from the USA with this idea of applying these fins, quite successfully I thought, and it didn't do the car any harm.

Tim's appearance in the styling department was always something of a mystery. We were never really quite sure why Tim was there and what his connection was. He didn't really seem to report in the way that we did to Ted White, and therefore we always thought there was some other kind of tie in to the Rootes family.

As the initial styling work on the Arrow saloon wound down, Rex moved on to design the estate car version. I was summoned into Ted's office and was told that they were going to replace the Sunbeam Rapier with a design based on the Arrow. I was told this was my project to lead and I was to do everything that was necessary to bring the Rapier to fruition.

This was my breakthrough, as it were, into a position of responsibility leading a small team of designers to put this vehicle together. My responsibility was for both the interior and exterior and it was quite a significant thing because it was around this time that Chrysler started to take a real interest in Rootes.

5

The Sunbeam Rapier: 1965–1967

THIS WAS THE FIRST PROJECT I had full control of, and I was given the responsibility to develop the Rapier as a derivative of the Arrow project. Most of the staff in the studio worked on the project for me part time and we started with sketches, following these with a quarter scale model.

The work was restricted by a carry-over formula. Rootes was certainly not flush with cash at that time and was struggling to do the project at all. I was given a formula to work with: the entire floorpan, firewall and mechanical components all would be carried over from the Arrow (now called the Hunter). That included, on the exterior of the vehicle, the whole front end. Certainly, the front wings would be carry-over but the tail lights, amazingly enough, had to carry over from something in the range, as well as did the outer wheel arch, which was in two pieces outer and inner.

That created a major restriction, as the Rapier was a two-door car, as distinct from the Hunter. The front wing carry-over meant that the side section was dictated from front to rear by that front wing though the outer panels from the A pillar to the rear were all new because of the two-door configuration. Also, the rear wheel arch size was dictated by the outer wheel arch carry-over, and the tail lights would obviously have some effect whichever ones were chosen.

For the first quarter scale models, I only have photographs of the model I did, but I do not recall that anyone else did a Rapier exterior as the others were working on the interior. My model was made to the carry-over formula, and everything was predictable as a result. I chose to use a fastback design, which was a departure from the previous Rapier, which had a notchback and a wraparound rear window.

Initial Rapier design, and already Roy Axe was told it was impossible to build because of the wrap-around rear window. At this stage it also had a multiplicity of Arrow carry-over parts.

However, in my model, I did keep the wraparound one-piece window feature. On the fastback car, the rear window came over the sides of the car, to line up with the belt line. The tail lights were from the Arrow estate because they offered the greatest visual difference from the Hunter saloon, and they fitted the side section.

The small scale model went ahead and received a lot of enthusiasm. However, as it evolved, the feasibility group (the engineers that is), informed me quite pointedly that it was not possible to have a back light (window) of that size all in one piece. This was because the corners would have such a large radius that it would not be possible to achieve what I was looking for.

I hadn't anything really to fight them with, as this was technical information, which actually originated from Triplex, our glass supplier. The only real solution to this problem was to divide the rear window into three pieces, so that the glass that was on the side of the car was quite separate, a quarter light in effect.

Because this was a two-door car there was already a quarter light in the side window area, as the window extended rearward of the door. This led to what was a multiplicity of pillars around the car. That wasn't really my favourite feature of the vehicle, but unfortunately I couldn't do what I wanted to do.

Ironically, many people have often asked me, were we aware when we did this car of the Barracuda design in the USA? The answer to that is no, we were categorically not informed of that project. The Barracuda did have a one-piece rear window. This would have been valuable information for me, though in truth, the radius achieved would probably have still been too large for our project as we had a much narrower car to work with.

Any really new project in the USA was kept close to Chrysler's chest. It should be remembered that Chrysler merely had some form of interest in Rootes at that time, and

Rapier dashboard proposal was also restricted by carry-over requirements.

we were making no visits to the USA. We did have a visit from Colin Neal over from Chrysler, as the Rapier entered the full-size model stage. But Colin did not try to change or force any great influence on the Rapier model.

Colin Neal was, however, very helpful in the design of the fascia (dashboard), for the Rapier, not only because he had responsibility for the international studio in Detroit, but also for interior design and therefore he was in a position to put in a number of suggestions for the interior of the car, specifically the instrument panel and fascia.

We did produce a number of fascia designs in-house, but they were restricted by the carry-over formulas again and by requirements that the engineers had, although it has to be said that the input from Detroit was also from a different direction, it offered a different approach, and it was something we all liked.

Sketches were sent over and we saw their designs as a way of getting something more advanced than we were able to produce. Our limitations were engineering ones, but we were also limited by our own imagination. Colin sent over a few designs and we chose one that could be developed into a model to try and make it fit the packaging.

The pressure to do something that Detroit had suggested was quite high, though this was not a forced situation. The design was better than ours and we made the decision to go with it. Therefore, we had strength to our arm in our battles with engineering, and we were in a better position to argue our case with the engineers this time round.

The design chosen by us from those that came over was, essentially, the one that ended up in the car, and which remained in the car for its whole life. It was quite a simple form, with a cut-out shape around the steering wheel and column, with the instruments set lower down. It was simple, effective, we all liked it and we were able to fit it to the package, and get it to work inside the car as well. The design was integrated with our own design for the door, the seats and all the other interior details.

With the steering wheel, we were unable to use the popular, until then, aluminium spokes for safety reasons but we still tried to get the look of a metal spoked wheel by adding inserts into the plastic wheel spokes. But believe me, it was no easy task to get things like that through engineering feasibility at the time.

The thing that did really concern me was the carry-over formula and the way it influenced the side of the car. It looked deep sided, was very upright in the vertical section, and was not very adventurous at all. It did not flatter the car and it did not emphasise the length, but it certainly emphasised the height up to the waistline.

My argument was for new front wings, which, I pointed out, would not only free up the side section

Rapier with Arrow front wings was less than successful – extra money was needed for a greater number of bespoke panels.

of the vehicle, but also give us more scope for individuality across the front.

I argued very strongly, this being the first chance I had in my career of being in the lead position to argue for something like this. I produced a sketch to better put this argument across. The new side section I proposed was fuller, and had a single crease line from front to rear just above the wheel arches.

At the rear, it lined up with the angled tail lights from the estate car. It all fitted in very smoothly and achieved a much more pointed, pleasant front end to the car, and by putting a V shape in plan view on the bonnet we were able to get a distinct V shape and movement into the front end, too.

At that time, I would also have liked to have changed the tail lights for something else, because the one disadvantage of the estate car tail lights, which were angled forward from mid point to the top, was that that created a rear end that was rather difficult to handle in terms of the shape that then projected across the rear of the vehicle.

There was a third thing I wanted to do too: to enlarge the outer wheel arch at the rear, so that the rear wheel was exposed more and wider wheels could be fitted. The Hunter wheel arch actually came quite low over the wheel and while that wasn't a real problem on the saloon it was on the Rapier. The Rapier would have been much better without the visual 'weight' between the top of that wheel arch and the beltline.

The upshot of this after a great deal of discussion, and the Rootes family almost bursting into tears at the thought of having to spend more money on the new items, was that I was given the concession that the front wing could be new. This therefore gave me the scope on the bonnet and the front end and really clinched the side of the car. It's ironic that after achieving nearly all-new sheet metal throughout the whole of this car, we were still dictated to by the carry-over of the tail lights.

That was really short-sighted because I think the cost involved would have been relatively minuscule and it would have made a very large difference to the rear end of the vehicle as it was produced.

Similarly I was also refused permission to change the rear wheel arch which was also a relatively very small cost and which would have changed the car considerably at the rear; it would have lightened it up and given it a more distinctive look.

However, I had to be thankful for small mercies and the front wing change was a major plus which gave the car quite a different look from the Hunter.

Everything was an enormous struggle, and it seemed to us often so frustrating. I would often

Full-scale Rapier modelling, and that three-piece window. Just about all of the panels were now new, barring the Arrow estate rear lamp clusters.

look at something that the Italians did, because I was greatly influenced by their designs. Sometimes they'd make me feel like I was banging my head against the wall because we were fighting for something that the Italians did on some car or another that went way beyond what we were trying to do.

Even the Americans were able to do things that we were not able to do because their styling departments had become their *design* departments, incorporating a design engineering function. They had a lot more clout in terms of what they were able to make happen. That wasn't always good as in some cases the designs that were proposed in the USA were so difficult to manufacture that this in itself made the quality of manufacture secondary, as the production feasibility had not been properly worked out.

These were cases where the styling of a car had an adverse affect on the quality but essentially if you look at what was being done in the USA during the 1950s and '60s, in terms of complexity of shapes, it's just mind-boggling. The shapes, the forms, the castings, the fins that came along, all of those absolutely OTT features resulted in cars that we'll never see the likes of again.

Some people will say 'thank God', but most of us view it as unfortunate in a way because the cars had undeniably great character. I live in the USA now and attend many cars shows and look at all these magnificently preserved cars, from the '40s to the '60s, and it just blows my mind that these things could be done, and that they could be actually sold for a very low price. Design had a very strong hold over these cars, or more precisely, style did and the American public enthusiastically gobbled all this up.

However, that is not what happened with the Rapier, which was quite refined for its time, and quite simple. I think with additional changes in the areas I have mentioned, the Rapier could have been a very much more effective car. If the track had been wider, it would have looked really so much better. I recall a company Rapier that I had for a while, that I had with wider wheels fitted.

There was a rear wheelarch clearance problem and it would not have been possible to do that in production for chain clearance purposes. This was caused by the restriction of the carry-over outer wheelarch. The engineers obviously had to have some limits somewhere and the restriction on this for production and legislative requirements was real but a new wheelarch would have solved the problem.

Later in the Rapier's life, a version called the H120 was fitted with the wider wheels and looked all the better for it. Unfortunately, the whole thing was just carried too far in those early stages and the styling clout wasn't there to push new ideas ahead. That was to come in the post 1967 days, when we effectively had the influence in the styling department by having the Americans behind us.

It should be said though that Chrysler was a very conservative company too, and we were still restricted relative to the competition. But it started a movement that would evolve through to a time when a lot of the sacred cows of engineering were thrown out, and there was able to be a much better balance between appearance and engineering.

The negative side of it was that in order to make that change we had to accept a lot of American direction. What the Americans were doing then became a great influence on what we were about to do, not all of it good!

We had this problem that we had no way to challenge the engineering due to the reporting line management structure. Engineering gave us a package that was virtually impossible to change. They also had a book of restrictions that was a bible and written almost as long ago and so we could only do what it said even though common sense told us on occasion that there had to be a better way.

Chrysler had had this problem too and was one of, if not the last, company in the USA to establish an engineering presence in Styling. This group could challenge the engineers with another view with the objective of improving the look of the product. With Chrysler advising us we were able to have a body engineer from the Chrysler design department, Ted Busch, attached to our department to help in this regard, with quite fierce opposition from engineering of course.

Later a British engineer was assigned to us for a while, but when the new reporting situation of Chrysler UK came into effect we had a small group established as styling engineers led by Arthur Long who was a respected member of body engineering. This

An interesting studio project to take the Arrow upmarket – by stretching its rear.

enabled us to challenge engineering where needed and later take a major role in the packaging of the car before styling work commenced. All this is normal practice today, but it really had to be fought hard for then.

That was the strength of engineering in those days, styling was viewed an important but it was something that was superficial. It was something that should be applied to the basic engineering package. Engineering was something 'scientific' that could be quantified. In fact many restrictions were there because the engineers said that they had to be and it was very difficult to challenge that.

In most cases, the Rootes family themselves were loath to change anything that had a stated engineering limitation to it because they were obviously afraid that the product would not perform as it should in the market and that would be a major problem.

After considerable debate between all interested parties, the changes to the package of the Rapier were agreed and the design was then progressed straight from quarter-scale to full-size. The styling theme was carried over completely into full-size, and it was a short programme that went relatively smoothly. I was generally pleased with the outcome.

So what would I have done with the Rapier given fewer carry-overs? No problem with the floorpan, and the basic shape, I'm happy with that. I would have certainly done more to increase the size of the wheelarches because it was extremely important to reduce the effect of the heaviness in the rear quarters. Pushing the track outwards would have had a very good effect too, so getting the outside of the tyres in a much better relationship with the sides of the body, and put a little more plan shape in the vehicle in the process.

Those were things that would have definitely been done given the chance. I would also have made the rear window the one-piece piece of glass I wanted it to be, I would have given the vehicle tumblehome on the sides, and more rake on the windscreen. And of course change the tail lights to something new to give us some flexibility back there. If all of those things had been done, I think the Rapier would have been a much more striking car than it was, although it has to be said it was well received in the market.

The Rapier had its disappointments but I don't think I've worked on any car that, in retrospect, would not have looked better given a few changes. That's just the cross the designer has to bear, I suppose.

This was at a time that the continuation of the Tiger was also being looked at. The Tiger had a Ford engine, which was unacceptable to Chrysler – but the Chrysler V8 would not fit in an engine bay.

There was a lot of two-dimensional work done by the International Studio in Chrysler Detroit, which was for a Tiger II development, a car to follow on if Chrysler wanted it. We also did work on the Tiger II in the UK.

The stretch idea was extended and modernised in order to produce a contemporary looking replacement ...

The programme was deemed unprofitable regrettably and the Alpine/Tiger was allowed to die.

Something else important happened in this period of time, our son Christopher was born. We were then living in a suburb of Coventry and my wife Pat had decided to have the baby at home. Being a midwife herself, she was well aware of what this entailed and had arranged for the appropriate midwife support to be available when required. As with the birth of my daughter Jane, Pat left things to the last moment; a degree of professional pride involved here!

When the moment did arrive, we were in the middle of a quite severe snowstorm and the midwife was having great difficulty getting to us. This was not my scene but I think I did a reasonable job of masking the animal panic I was feeling. The midwife finally arrived and only just in time, a great relief all round ...

At this time, our very tired Mini had to go. This was one of the few times we have really felt an emotional tug when disposing of a car. The Mini had served us well but something newer was needed.

We bought one of the new Hillman Imps, and despite its reputation for unreliability, we had a very good experience with this car. It was a much better vehicle than the Mini, from personal experience of both. It was a nimble and comfortable little car and served us very well. Later on Pat had a couple of Imp coupés, attractively styled again by Bob Saward, which we liked too and which gave us good service.

If the problems of the Imp's reliability had not been there and also the problems of the Scottish build fiasco, this could have been a very successful car. But the car world was also becoming besotted with transverse front wheel drive then so perhaps the poor old Imp was doomed anyway.

6

Rootes – The Decline and Enter Chrysler: 1967

THE ROOTES FAMILY WAS very autocratic. It ran the business with an iron fist and people who were in the senior positions met their requirements without too much argument. Rootes was battling difficult circumstances post 1960; it had a declining business in terms of profit, and made some decisions that didn't work out. These included a crippling strike at BLSP (British Light Steel Pressings), that the Rootes family didn't give way to, eventually forcing the operation to go out of business.

The second thing was the government forced Rootes to build its new factory for the Imp in Scotland in an area of low employment. Rootes was not the only company to suffer, because they forced British Leyland to build plants in places not traditionally familiar with the car industry. Though these were nobly intended to increase employment in those areas, it was a disaster in the long term.

Rootes needed a new car to attract younger buyers, and that was achieved in the production of the Imp, an attractive and revolutionary car; however, being assembled in Scotland at Linwood hampered the Imp. The problem with this was that various components were transported from Coventry to Scotland, on specially dedicated trains. Then the completed cars were shipped back to the Midlands to be delivered; overall it was something of a fiasco.

Some stamping was done at Linwood but a lot of materials were taken up there and, as the Imp was the smallest car with the lowest selling price in the Rootes range, it was the least profitable. These costs manifested themselves into disastrously low returns and the end result was increased financial difficulty for Rootes, which eventually caused the sell-out to Chrysler.

The Rootes family ran a very tight ship. As designers, we were low down the totem pole, because we reported to Engineering. This was not to the Director of Engineering but the head of body design, George Payne, who then reported up the Engineering hierarchy to the Director, BB Winter. We were way down the pecking order, and when it came down to the availability of supplies and materials to do our work, it was a real struggle. Pencils were in great demand, paper, sketch pads, things like that were like gold dust and it really was a very difficult environment from that point of view.

Today's designers would in no way recognise the difficulties we had to go through. This was all very problematic and caused a lot of resentment at the way we had to do our work. It also bought a great deal of camaraderie; we were all in the same boat and all had to work together with a great deal of good will and humour. Salaries were low, and increases became more difficult as the company became less profitable. All of these things were hard to cope with. Nevertheless I look back at those days as good times.

Turning to how this affected car design, the Minx was the stalwart product of the group, simple and relatively cheap to produce and it was profitable. As is the case with most companies, the model in the popular area of the market is the real bread and butter, a key product and one that you have to get right to be profitable, as Ford demonstrated with the Cortina and Escort.

There were other things that we, as designers, knew we could do to improve the appearance of the cars, but these were still out of court, largely again down to Engineering. The key ones were the position of the cant rail relative to the driver's head. The Italians were admired for style and their cars had a great deal more tumblehome; that is the way the side leans in from the waistline to the top of the door. This gave a more rakish look, however, the engineers felt that there needed to be a great deal more distance between the driver's head and the side rail inside the car, otherwise it would have seemed quite claustrophobic to the passengers.

Similarly with the windscreen angle, that was severely limited in the amount of rearward rake you could put on the windscreen because the top of that windscreen would then come uncomfortably close to the eyes. There was also the issue that if a windscreen leaned back beyond a certain angle, the driver would not be able to see through it because of the distortion looking forward. All of these limitations were later proved unnecessary, and cars have now benefited by adopting more flexible rules.

Chrysler started to show an interest in purchasing Rootes, and had already acquired Simca in France, and Barrieros, a truck manufacturer, in Spain. Both GM and Ford had European subsidiaries dating from pre-WW2, but Chrysler had remained a strictly American manufacturing company. It first acquired an interest in Simca and then Rootes and soon after that, the first of the people from the USA arrived in the UK to act as advisers and make some helpful suggestions.

The first man from Chrysler to be assigned to Rootes was Bob Kushler. He was with us for more than a year, or so as I recall. He was an engineer and his role was to be attached to the engineering function. As such, he had a great deal to do with Harry Sheron, who had developed the Arrow, and was then the senior man in Engineering at that time. Bob was able to shed light on quite a few things that Chrysler did, or had in progress.

Of course he had come from an engineering environment and it wasn't until Virgil Exner produced his 'finned' cars, that we started to see a real advance in the styling work at Chrysler. Engineering was the dominant factor in Chrysler and Chrysler cars were viewed as 'well engineered' if a little stodgy. Bob was educated in the Chrysler Institute, a University level educational facility, which turned out engineers for the company and they did it the Chrysler way.

They were all dedicated Chrysler men and had risen to senior management posts. Their feelings were very strong in terms of what the company could and couldn't do. They saw at Rootes, what I am sure seemed to them to be, a very primitive operation. There were some spirited arguments and I had clashes with Bob in terms of what we could and could not do in terms of feasibility.

He was a very forceful personality, but did form strong and helpful associations with some people in the engineering department. Bob was very helpful overall and opened our eyes to many things. He was a nice guy, always well turned out and very polite; always nice to me, despite our disagreements at times. It is fair to say that Bob and Stan Taylor, one of the senior Rootes body engineers and the one responsible for the Imp body, did not hit it off too well.

Bob related better to Dick Newman, who was at a similar level in the body engineering operation to Stan and Dick and who had done much work on the Tiger and Alpine body engineering.

Dick was a guy that I also enjoyed the company of and he was perhaps a little more relaxed emotionally than Stan. I travelled with Dick a few times to Italy when we were involved over there. There was this slightly uncomfortable triangle in body engineering involving Bob Kushler, but I think overall, Bob's time at Rootes was a considerable eye opener to all of us.

For a while before he retired, he was in my styling operation at Chrysler in the USA in charge of the administration part of the operation. He lives not too far away from us in Florida now so we do meet from time to time to reminisce.

Colin Neal was the first Chrysler man from Styling to come over to visit. He was accomplished in design, working on the Consul and Zephyr for Ford in the UK, then going to the USA following the relationship he had formed with the people there. He was someone who related well to Elwood Engel, then a senior man at Ford USA styling. When Elwood moved out of Ford and replaced Virgil Exner as Design VP at Chrysler he took Colin with him to run the Interior Design operations at Chrysler.

Colin also ran the International Studio at Chrysler and he could have done two things when he came over to visit us in the UK. He could have used his background, knowledge and connections at Chrysler to overwhelm us in no time at all, or he could take the approach of being a constructive teacher and help us with what we were doing.

I'm glad to say that he took the latter course and he was very helpful. He was clearly on a different experience plane to us, as stylists, at the time. But that was advantageous to us, we were very keen to learn and it was that relationship that was so helpful to me and was the platform from which I was put into a more senior role in the Chrysler European operation later on.

Looking back, this was a very interesting time. A lot of things were happening, with many more about to. I had taken on a lot of extra responsibilities.

At work, the responsibility of taking the leadership of designing things and making them work was a totally new experience for me. Through the early stages of my design career, I had been avidly keen on Italian cars; they have always held a great fascination for me in terms of shapes and proportion.

Starting before the war, and carrying on after, there were some truly spectacular designs produced in Italy. During the 1961–67 period I had the opportunity to broaden my horizons and visit some of the international motor shows. These were expansive visits lasting three–four days, with quite a few people going. The Rootes family was usually pretty generous on these sorts of things, and we got a good chance to spend lots of time to examine these exotic foreign cars.

The Turin auto show was always a highlight, although I did get to Geneva and Paris during this particular period of time; but it was the Italian show that really excited me. Rootes was developing some cars that had the Italians involved, and the two that became serious projects were the Zimp, which was developed from the Imp by Zagato. Also there was a version of the Humber Sceptre, the Venezia, which was developed in Italy by Touring.

Dick Newman and I had the opportunity to visit these coachbuilders, when these vehicles were under development. I also had the chance to visit other coachbuilders, as we usually did a tour around while we were at the show, visiting Bertone, Pininfarina, Ghia and some of the smaller ones, a very interesting and inspiring experience.

The very best artisans were employed by Pininfarina, Bertone of course, and Touring and Ghia as well, because they had the biggest customer base, and they were dealing with customers who were paying them large sums of money.

It was very interesting to see the cars that were being produced in the Italian shops. There was less secrecy back then, and we could see the show cars being worked on. It was fascinating to see the contrast between the more affluent operations, and Zagato, for example.

It was a small company, producing a smaller number of vehicles and consequently they could not charge as much for the product as some of the others, and the quality of the panel beater's work was not as good as those employed by Bertone and Pininfarina.

The end result was that a body by Zagato before paint looked something like a copper kettle. The finish came with lead-loading, which was not a very healthy process, and also one that involved almost styling the car in lead, not to mention the weight which must have been added!

This must have been a nightmare for repairing a damaged car, as it didn't just mean bolting on another panel, but it was necessary to virtually restyle the car with the lead-loading to match the original shapes!

The Zagato brothers were a charming pair in the best Italian tradition, and the younger one did all the entertaining, showing us what they were doing as work on the Zimp progressed. It was a two-door coupé based on the Imp, and quite interesting. But it did not proceed in the end for commercial reasons.

The Zagato brothers were enthusiastic and tried hard to get our business. One day we went out to lunch with them, and it went well as lunches in Italy seem to go! Our host suddenly realised it was too late for us to get to the airport.

We were in Milan, we had to go round the ring road to the airport, and this particular Zagato brother had been a racing driver, and quite capable of driving briskly when required.

We set off in a Lancia Fulvia Zagato Coupé and away we went at high speed, myself, Dick Newman and with Mr Zagato driving. We had a very eventful trip to the airport. In fact, we were involved in five minor accidents or incidents of one kind or another. In one, we were approaching traffic lights, the idea being the lights would have changed when we got there.

They didn't and there was a car already standing there, which we overtook on the inside, on the sidewalk, taking off his front bumper. There was a lot of waving out of windows, and away we went, carrying on for the airport. There were a few of these sorts of incidents, including one very high speed run down the last section of highway going into the airport when we passed a police car and to our amazement nothing happened.

When we pointed this out to Mr Zagato, he said that we were in an expensive car, and the police were never quite sure who the owner would be. Therefore there would be no problem.

We arrived at the airport, but just missed our flight, which was mortifying to Mr Zagato who insisted on waiting with us until the next flight took off quite a while later.

We felt bad having him sitting around but he felt that was what he had to do as that was how business was conducted in those days, and people cared about such details.

We also went to Touring to see the Venezia. It was a very nice car, produced at the end of the company's life, sadly, as this once great company had fallen on hard times, and was almost out of business. Although some Venezias were produced for the Italian market, it was not long after that when Touring went out of business completely.

A great pity, as I think this was a company that was very influential on the design of cars in their pre-war work, and also post-war when they produced some stunning designs such as the Ferrari 166 Barchetta, which was an icon of its day. The designer of that car was Carlo Anderloni, who was a very charming and talented gentleman.

Back in Coventry, and after the completion of the Sunbeam Rapier, we were given the Avenger programme to do. Although I had a lead role in the project there was a lack of cohesion in the team. Tim Fry was working separately and no one knew exactly where he fitted in the grand scheme of things. There were a number of models made, and a few in full-size with a model I had done being the leading contender.

During this period, Tim was suddenly dispatched to Chrysler's International studio in Detroit. There was no explanation to us, or to Ted White, but we all felt that when Tim came back he would take over from Ted.

Work on the models proceeded, and after a couple of months or so, Tim returned with Elwood, together with a full-size model of an Avenger to present to us.

This model had been completed in the International Studios, and was very well finished with a theme that was a kind of evolution of my proposal. But it had been influenced, we found out later, from the work being done in Detroit on their cars, which we were not allowed to see.

This was all in 1966. Elwood was a very much larger than life character, and he just overwhelmed everyone including the Rootes family and the senior management. The model did not conform to the limitations that we were working to, but that did not deter Elwood and the proposal was chosen on the spot.

This was also presented as Tim's work, which was not really the case. We all felt that the model was very good if a little too American, so we were not against it but it was now looking a sure thing that Tim was to be our new boss. Elwood had been very clever in using a member of the Rootes team in this way, though I do not think it was his idea to do that. The project was go with instructions to the engineers to not change anything.

The expected move to replace Ted with Tim did not take place straight away. Much to my surprise, I was called into Ted's office and told I was being sent to the USA, on what sounded a rather strange mission.

I was also being sent to Colin Neal's studio but there was no clearly identified project for me to do. I was really out there to work alongside the designers, get to know them and get a feel for the operation at Chrysler.

I was given a period of time, a sum of money and told to 'soak up the atmosphere'. I stayed in a local motel, and it was obvious to me that I was there to be observed.

This was the first time I'd been to the USA of course, and what happened there was such an education. Colin Neal, and I had liaised on the design of the Rapier interior, and we had accepted his design for the instrument panel of the Rapier, developing it in house from a sketch. Colin therefore, knew me, and he was instrumental in me being invited to go over there.

I went as a relatively junior individual, and Colin was on a level way above me, operating with the other directors of the studios at the time. My main contact was with people within the studio, for whom I developed a very healthy respect and in many cases a lasting friendship.

Hal Pilky was running the place, and Bill Dayton was in charge of the interiors side. Bill and I became good friends. Art Blakeslee was also in the studio at the time, and he'd eventually go on to replace me at Chrysler International in Europe in Whitley, Coventry.

There were other characters in there, such as Gerry Piaskowski. Gerry's name was the first American name to appear on a sketch to come across from Detroit, and the name fascinated us all at the time. Gerry and I remain good friends to this day. Bob Andrews was friendly to me, and he was a very interesting person because of his work with Raymond Loewy.

I was very impressed by the standard of the design that was going on in that studio. Most of the work was for Australia and South America, and it was most interesting to be there. When I first got to Detroit, modelling manager Len Klemick took me under his wing. He met me at the airport first time into the USA and drove me straight to the Chrysler studio, which at that time was located in Highland Park, and I was put into the hotel for the night.

I spent the remainder of the day being introduced to everyone, then was given a very large Plymouth car with instructions as to where the motel was and told to get on with it. I then drove to the motel not knowing where I really was but it all worked out in the end!

I managed to get down to Washington and Gettysburg with a bunch of Australians that were there, Mike Stacy being the man in charge. Mike was someone I also worked with later on, when dealing with the C-body for Australia.

I used the opportunity to visit Washington, and see my cousin Joan, who had married an American serviceman. Driving cars in the USA was an interesting experience. I usually had a fairly basic model to drive, but they all seemed huge and impressive to me at the time.

I was given a Barracuda, which of course is the car that has been likened to the Rapier. Put them side-by-side and there are plenty of differences; they both have a fastback, and both have wraparound rear windows admittedly, but they don't really carry-over any other styling features. The Barracuda was quite an impressive car in the USA at that time, and its huge back window was quite distinctive. I took it up to Niagara Falls for a weekend trip.

I remember one evening driving into downtown Detroit, down Woodward Avenue, when I missed a traffic light. Of course, the traffic lights in the USA are high up and in the centre of the road, a different location than in the UK. It was just my luck that there was a cop on the sidewalk, which was quite unusual even in those days. I missed the light and braked hard, and because American cars weren't that great in those conditions, I came to a halt in a large cloud of blue smoke broadside on at the light but luckily not going over the line.

There was a pregnant pause, I had my window down, and the cop strolled towards me. He withdrew his pistol first, which made me feel very uneasy, then turned it around and held it butt first, well out of my reach of course, and said 'Here bud try this, it's quicker', which I thought was an amusing way to tackle that problem. He did no more, and just put his gun away and walked off!

I did, of course, get to see the other studios at Chrysler. I was introduced to the other four design directors, and it was mind-boggling walking in to these huge studios with all the work proceeding on these truly vast cars.

There were station wagons, in clay, full-size, which were just huge, and it was hard to judge scale in that environment. But I managed this very quickly and although these cars were big, they didn't seem so much so when in context. Looking at them now (I often see the cars of that era when I attend car shows in the USA), the American cars of that era are still huge, complex and impressive.

7

Chrysler UK: 1967

THE ROOTES FAMILY HANDED over control to Chrysler in 1967, the year the Rapier was introduced. Chrysler took over the company, and added it to its growing European portfolio. When the takeover was announced, there was a complete revolution and the existing management was ousted. The Rootes family all but disappeared, except for Lord Rootes, who became the chairman, even if he was little more than a figurehead.

Gilbert Hunt became the MD of the Rootes Group, Harry Sheron became the Design Director, Ted White remained, but was promoted to the title of Styling Director. I was appointed to the position of Chief Stylist much to my considerable surprise. I was still a rather green 29-year-old!

Rex Fleming was appointed as the administrator of the styling operation. Rex had been sent to Detroit for a short time just after me, and clearly Rex and I were under observation for another nine months. After that, Ted White retired, and at that point I became the Director of Design for what then became Chrysler UK.

Once appointed, a further visit to Detroit was immediately arranged. I returned to the International Studio as the Chief Stylist of the Rootes studio, and although our facility wasn't even as big as the International operation in Detroit, it carried considerable status. All of a sudden I was meeting all the other people in the studios, having lunch, talking with them, meeting the personalities, all of whom were very friendly towards me.

Colin Neal was in charge of Interior design as well as International, Elwood Engel had moved him in from Ford. Engel had been overlooked to succeed George Walker as the Vice President of Ford, and Gene Bordinat got that position instead. Elwood was George's recommendation, which made things difficult at Ford so the end result was that

he joined Chrysler as Vice President of Design.

Design had clearly taken a big step up at Chrysler, and Elwood was a God-like figure at the top. Colin was helpful to me, friendly, never overwhelming, and considering his senior role within the organisation, this was surprising.

Bill Brownlee was in charge of the small/medium cars exteriors. He was a very dapper character, and very tough to deal with in a presentation if you happened to be presenting another point of view!

He was capable at making his point, and was a slick mover.

He had been responsible for the Dodge Charger, and had very strong contacts throughout Chrysler. Cliff Voss was Director of large car exteriors, and was the older guy in the operation, a very charming gentlemanly character who had been with Chrysler a long time. Dick McAdam, Director for Exterior design, was also another strong character. Everyone in the International studio was very friendly.

Colin's right hand man in Interior design was Tom Bingman. He was known as the 'Old Grouch', and was a meticulous designer, a keen eye, and a great expert on soft trim. Tom and I had a very close relationship for many years, as I will relate later on, and Tom was a very good friend to me through the next few years.

I've always been fascinated with the USA, I was keen on movies, and I used to visit the cinema in Scarborough to see all the early US films, with their fascinating cars. I was always an admirer of these cars and when I came face to face with Detroit, I found I had an even stronger positive feeling for the USA. I've always found myself comfortable in the USA and have a great empathy with Americans and that made my working relationship with those in Chrysler even more pleasurable.

This was a time when I made the transition from a drawing board designer to a design manager. This was a big step to make, a designer on the drawing board only needs to worry about the car, and often only parts of it. Managing a design team is a very different thing.

That extended to the Avenger project too. There was a great deal of work done on scale models, illustrations and the like, and in that early stage, I wasn't in charge of the project, merely contributing to it. The design parts of my responsibilities were in setting the direction for the vehicle concept at the beginning of the project. This is very important because sometimes there is not the focus there should be, and the design team can get off-course with much effort wasted.

There's always a limited amount of time to design a car in, and if you spend too much effort on directions that are too widely spread in the beginning then this time is wasted.

There is a need for focus, and the Design Director's job is to facilitate this, while also allowing the stylists to explore their own ideas within an envelope. If the Design Director

The idea of stretching the Avenger into a hatchback was nurtured during this period. It would have generated additional sales, but at what cost?

(DD) produces an illustration of what the direction should be, and tells his staff that is the way we're going to go (and there are a number of DDs who do this), it is very demoralising for the designers.

The important thing is balance and input from everyone but the goals must be firmly set and kept to. The DD must then guide the team along, with frequent viewings and discussions.

Finally, the design is refined, and resolved within the department. Then it is the DD's job, when he is satisfied, to present it to a management group consisting of the Directors of the company. This might be called a Design Committee or something of the sort, but the DD will present the design to them, and must convince them that this is the way to go. If the group disagrees, then he has to take a lead role in negotiating that design in a revised direction.

Another transition I went through was the increasing exposure to the motoring press. Even back then, there was a tremendous interest in the design side. Engineering to the general public was a little bit boring, so the styling was something the public could always relate to, and they were always interested in the process of how this design work was carried through.

Increasingly, I was projected as an interface with the press by the PR department. Generally speaking I found I got on very well with the press, and it was always a good relationship as far as I was concerned, despite the fact that many journalists were very devious in what was reported. There are not too many members of the press you can really trust to report exactly what was said in an interview, and one must always be on guard against an 'off the cuff' remark, and say things as they really are or 'no comment'.

It was sometimes a difficult relationship. I would go through a dialogue with an interviewer before going on camera, only to arrive in a situation that when the microphones and cameras were switched on the interviewer would ask about something completely different. Especially if there was some sort of scandal going on in the company even though it was nothing to do with the real subject of the interview. All very sneaky!

There are a few journalists who you can be close to in terms of discussing what is happening, knowing that those remarks are not going to get passed on unless you want them to be. Phil Llewellyn was probably the best journalist in this regard that I've ever known. He was a great enthusiast, and someone you could have a confidential conversation with about anything at all.

I had to do a lot of speaking at conventions and the like. The first experience I had of this was at Loughborough University to give a talk on how styling work was done on the Rapier project. With some pushing by the PR department, I reluctantly agreed to do it, and I gathered together a lot of material to be able to demonstrate how we worked taking a small scale model, and the tools we used plus sketch work and so on.

The university told me that this was a very intimate little group, and that I would be able to sit down in a very relaxed atmosphere and present all this. So I duly went to the meeting and just before it started, I was plied with a gin and tonic and given a lot of confidence boosting patter by the powers that be, and I was beginning to be slightly edgy about what was actually going on.

Eventually I was wheeled up to a set of double doors into the lecture theatre and it was announced to me as we walked through the door that there had been a great deal of interest in this talk after it was publicised in the university and 'oh, by the way, there are 200 plus people in the auditorium who are looking forward to what you have to say'! It was one of those tiered lecture rooms absolutely packed with people, and I was mentally unprepared for that experience.

If I'd been told beforehand, maybe I'd have been better prepared for the experience but maybe, in one way, it's a good thing to be pitched in at the deep end like that because I quickly realised I had to get on with it. I made the presentation, gave all the demonstrations and the whole thing was a roaring success.

That experience gave me a great deal of confidence for future speeches and meetings, in large groups, an interesting baptism of fire and a lasting lesson to always be prepared with good material at all times just in case.

8

Chrysler UK and Europe: 1968

BY THE MID 1960s, we had outgrown our design facilities at Rootes. We were located upstairs from the wood and pattern shop in Humber Road, and were really confined in terms of space, especially when it came to making clay models. The facility was designed to make full-sized wooden models downstairs, and quarter-scale Plasticine models upstairs.

In 1966 we extended out on to the adjacent flat roof and built a security wall to hide the outside viewing area from surrounding houses, and this created a modelling studio with an outside viewing area. It was still not very spacious but it was far, far better than before. That's how we went into 1967 after the Chrysler takeover. This was a true revolution, not only because of the increased space but also in the methods used to make models and develop projects.

We did have a hiring programme at this time, and we also lost a few people who had been around for quite a long time. Tom Firth went back to Ford, but Bob Saward remained. Between the two of them, they had brought the Rootes styling operation at least up to date in terms of technique. Modelling with clay, having a modelling manager, different design and sketching techniques and so on were all new to us.

In the post '67 period, this learning was expanded further; Chrysler introduced magic markers for sketching to us, for example, an advance from the coloured crayons we had been using up to that date, and the whole thing started to take off. In addition to Tom Firth leaving, there were others who went to new pastures. We had been operating under the Rootes family hierarchy, surnames only, of course. Everyone was careful how they addressed a member of the Rootes family, and we were really encouraged only to speak when spoken to.

Chrysler was the complete opposite. It was very friendly – first name terms for everyone – and we were encouraged to speak our minds, with everything on the table and in the open. Underneath it all, just like all American organisations, there is a very clear understanding as to who is who in an organisation.

Just because you address the chairman by his first name, you're not all buddy-buddy. But it was a much more friendly and personal atmosphere than before. Rootes was not unusual in the UK, it was just that the Chrysler/American way was very different – and we felt liberated!

It was a dramatic day when the company changed hands. Chrysler made some pretty sweeping announcements that affected all of us to a degree. And gone, literally overnight, was the previous hierarchical structure.

Gilbert Hunt was a suitably stylish MD, capable and very friendly, and obviously with a clear mandate from Chrysler. Equally obvious was that he was under the control of the Americans, and there was no doubt in any of our minds where the real power lay.

During this busy period, Chrysler pushed with sports car proposals.

Gilbert operated in a very refreshing and exciting way, creating a new organisation of people around him who reported to him. More importantly for us, was that he was a real enthusiast for style and had an instinct for its value on the marketplace.

Peter Ware had gone too, and in his place, in charge of all product development was Cyril Weighell. Cyril was a very nice person; gentle and approachable but with a big responsibility. He was chosen because of his willingness to delegate and allow the individual departments under his control to operate in their own way. He was the leader of the team.

Harry Sheron became the Engineering Director, and Ted White became the Styling Director – and an all-new position was created, Product Planning Director, with Bill Papworth being appointed into that post. Bill came from Ford and set up something that was very familiar to the Chrysler Corporation, but which was very new for the Rootes Group.

Concept for the 1970 London Motor Show – and sports cars were clearly seen as integral in Chrysler's future product plans.

This was a very significant thing for the styling organisation, because Ted White now reported directly to Cyril Weighell, although, in the Chrysler tradition, the Product Development boss was still an engineer. At Chrysler, Styling had become Design, and had moved into an independent reporting position accountable to the Product Development chief.

Elwood Engel may have been the

Another radical-looking sports car proposal.

first in that position in Chrysler though Virgil Exner, his predecessor, had been a VP and on the Board. Ted White became the styling director, I became the chief stylist for Rootes, and Rex Fleming became the admin boss for the organisation. It was an interesting situation, as Rex had design responsibility for the Hunter, and I'd had the responsibility for the Rapier, with each of us leading a part of the styling department.

Someone at the top clearly felt that I should be chosen to lead the whole design team, and I think Rex was in that position as a back up in case anything went wrong with my performance. Ted remained in the Director's spot but took a back seat role, and my relationship with him remained well, as I came to appreciate the difficulties he had been working under. He was also very helpful to me, giving me excellent advice.

He remained in the background and certainly didn't interfere, and I was being given the green light to take this thing by the scruff of the neck and make it work. All this was very exciting. In retrospect, that level of responsibility and the experience would scare the living daylights out of me today, but these people have an insight into people's potential, and I was given an opportunity that I grasped.

Ted White was greatly relieved by all these moves. Tim had been working in the department, but in reality he had a direct line into the Rootes family, and Peter Ware, and simply bypassed Ted White when it came to work assignments. Tim left the company and he went into something that was absolutely perfect for him, he established a company called Small Fry. It was a clever name, because he was anything but small in stature and personality, and the company developed ideas and inventions, and Tim was a clever guy at such things.

He established his business in Dunchurch near Coventry, and he remained there until few years ago, when he tragically died at a relatively early age. Another leaver at that time was William Towns. Bill and I had a close working relationship for some time, and we worked together as friendly competitors, until he eventually left to go and work for Rover.

He went to work for David Bache, where he stayed until he eventually left and joined Aston Martin. He was always an extremely enthusiastic and likeable guy and very competitive.

Later, when I was working in Detroit, I guess he came into some sort of inheritance and established a design consultancy out at Stretton-on-Dunsmore. He was in that business until he too died tragically at an early age. He was best known for his work at Aston Martin – his design work there was very much in his own style. He was into angular shapes and forms.

Much work was done on a further Sunbeam Tiger update, but once it became clear the Chrysler V8 engine wouldn't fit, the project was dropped.

There were some new starters, one of whom was Jim Hirons, who went on later to work at Ford. I remember when Elwood Engel came over to show the Avenger to the management; Jim buttonholed him pretty hard to try to get a position at Chrysler in the USA. Unfortunately all that came to nought as far as Jim was concerned, and I don't think Elwood was impressed by the approach.

Mike Moore joined the studios, coming from the Rootes training scheme just as I had done. One of the reasons why I latched onto him so strongly was that he was a very capable and practical designer. In those days there was a competition run by IBCAM for design, and quite a few well-known people won the prizes. Colin Neal won a prize, and so did Tom Karen, who eventually went on to run Ogle Design.

I got an honourable mention on the one time I did enter. It was a good competition, and by the time we had got to the late 1960s, it had changed so that it was a competition for a design, which if chosen, would be built as a running prototype.

A few of the winners' cars were built. Mike Moore was one of the people who entered it, won and had his car made for him. He eventually went to Chrysler in the USA before I did, and our paths crossed again when he became a member of my staff in interiors after my move to the USA.

I liked Mike a lot, and he certainly knew how to design cars. What happened to the car that was built for him I really don't know, maybe Mike still has it, but I think it remained in the UK but I lost touch with him except for an annual Christmas card exchange.

Coming the other way was Curt Gwinn. He was a Chrysler designer who came from Oregon. I had asked the people in Detroit to recommend a designer who would be suitable to move into our studio to widen our experience, and it was Curt they suggested.

He was the first American to work in our styling office, and in those days there were no real transfers on American salaries, so he had to accept the UK terms of employment and salary. This must have seemed pretty risible at the time.

Curt came over on the Queen Mary and I remember going to meet him in Southampton on a very dark and misty night. The QM came in appearing out of the gloom, which was an impressive sight. Curt came ashore, and we duly tried to find a hotel. I guess I didn't have one booked being a little green about such things in those days! When we found a hotel after quite a search, we had to share a room, which was all rather embarrassing!

We worked well together for a long time, and when I later left for the USA, Curt remained in the UK eventually to work for Peugeot. He then went over to France, learned French and became the Director for the Advanced Studio over there at Talbot. This was when Art Blakeslee ran the Peugeot studios.

Curt carried on with that job until retirement, and he was a very capable designer, and a major asset in the late 1960s.

Another guy who came over was Roger Zremec, who was also looking to get European experience, and was willing to take a European salary. He was a very useful addition, and the skills the pair had had were very much in the American manner, with a very good level of input.

We learned a lot from them, and it was good to have them aboard. Roger went back to the USA, taking my secretary with him, who he then married and who then tragically died. Roger eventually became the head of the Mitsubishi advanced studios in California, and the last time I saw him, on a visit I made there a few years ago, he was just the same guy. He has since left Mitsubishi.

The Chrysler UK Product Planning operation was something new to us. It operated somewhere between engineering and design. Very frequently PP would take the line for appearance rather than functionality so, when it came to applying more tumblehome on the superstructure, or more rake on the windscreen, we had help to fight the case.

Whereas engineering had the very strict parameters in the Rootes operation that you could not modify at all, there was quite a strong support from PP and Marketing and Sales to move into something more in keeping with the times.

Chrysler in the USA was extremely supportive of such things as well. It could still not do a lot of the things that we can do today in styling, such as placing road wheels to the outer edge of the bodywork, or dictating proportion to a degree. Chrysler Design could do things we could not do, and all that was quite exciting as this was what we wanted to do in the UK. Under Chrysler, all the things I would have liked to do with the Rapier would have been possible.

The PP department had the responsibility to propose cars that the company should have for the future, and evaluate the cost of such proposals with the finances available. From there, it could create a product plan that we could all work to – instead of the knee-jerk reaction of someone saying 'what should we do next?'

Bill Papworth brought in two younger guys to run the operation, Marc Honore and David Allen.

Marc Honore was important because he became a close colleague and friend, too. I don't see David Allen much these days, but Marc Honore and our families were very close, and our children grew up together. Though these days, he and his wife live in France, and we live in the USA, and we are still in touch.

Mark and I both ended up doing a vast amount of travel around the world, and we travelled together frequently. It was good that we got on well and that bode well for the future.

9

Chrysler International: 1968

THE TIME BETWEEN CHRYSLER taking over Rootes to the formation of Chrysler International Europe (CISA) was very active. Chrysler International was originally based in Geneva, and was created to integrate the three European companies into a single product planning and development entity.

Chrysler sent over George Gibson to establish the operation. The ex-head of Product Planning in Detroit, George was an interesting character who brought over quite a number of people from the USA. Some were questionable as to suitability, but others really proved their value.

Joe Farnham came over at that time in charge of quality, but he later moved to Chrysler France as head of R&D. Another engineer was Bob Sinclair, who had preceded Joe to France. Others were Joe Mallus and Dave Logan, who were at Simca. Bob Kushler had, by then, returned to the USA.

After a year Ted White retired. He had a difficult private life, his son was seriously mentally disabled, and it was tough for him. It took a while to realise this was the situation Ted was in, as he didn't talk about it to us at that time. Ted guided me along in this period and showed me how to run the department. It is amazing that so much trust was placed in such a relatively inexperienced group.

I will leave the reader to judge if this was a smart move, and created new thinking, or if it would have been better to leave a highly experienced group do this job. As it was, it turned out to be a good combination of American experience and a new way of doing things with the advantage of local talent to show that they were open to ideas from the locals.

At Simca, one of Chrysler's key product development executives, Harry Chesborough, arrived. He was an important man as he had been in charge of product development in the USA, and a thorn in the side of Elwood Engel. He was opinionated, especially about styling.

I remember showing him one of my styling models for the Chrysler 180 coupé at Whitley. The car had a sweeping belt line that dipped in the middle, a very common feature today.

He told me that no car with anything but a straight

Chrysler 180 coupé: spot the straight line ...

belt line would ever be successful anywhere! A definite statement and one that proved absolutely and utterly wrong in the following years of course.

Harry took over the operations in France, becoming the President of what would become Chrysler France, on the retirement of Georges Hereil. A degree of re-organising would then be needed, with Bob Sinclair becoming the Engineering Director, and Dave Logan his right hand man.

Bob Anders was brought over to become the Styling Director to replace Claude Geneste, who had not been in place that long. He was a nice man, but couldn't stand up to the high rollers in Chrysler France, and was certainly no match for the marketing department, which was truly formidable in Chrysler France.

Bob had been an interior design chief for Colin Neal, at one of the studios in Detroit, and he was brought over to run the design operation in France. He was charming privately, and an absolutely wonderful witty character to be with, but in business he was very different, tough to work with and very starchy.

Bob later became one of my chief designers when I moved across to the USA, so our paths crossed again. A designer called Irv Ritchie was brought in to oversee the Chrysler Europe Group in Geneva, and he was the design representative for International, spending his time going between Bob Anders' studio in France and mine. I was not sure what he was supposed to do and neither was Bob.

Irv really didn't make any kind of positive impression, and I don't know why he was sent over, one of a number of bad choices at that time. It was symptomatic of the time that not all the people Chrysler sent over were outstanding; most were experienced, but some were not a good choice at all.

The feeling we had was that these were people that Chrysler wanted off the scene, which was the worst of reasons for shipping them to Europe. We needed good people. Irv was someone whose face, perhaps, didn't totally fit in the USA, because he certainly had no basic attributes that I could see that would stand him in good stead in the job he was doing. He was a fish totally out of water!

A new larger car was required in the UK, and a lot of work went into what was to become the Chrysler 180. It was known as the C Body, with the Avenger being the B Body. At the bottom end of the range was the Imp, and no one quite knew what to do with that.

We did do a few studies on the Imp ranging from a sports car known as the Asp, which Tim Fry had worked on, through to other ideas, such as a mini MPV with forward control inspired by the Fiat Multipla.

The Imp was in difficulties because of quality but there was enthusiasm in some quarters, to do something more with it. Another car that there was enthusiasm to do something with was the Tiger, which was well acclaimed and was exciting to drive, largely due to its inferior roadholding.

We did numerous studies in the UK and USA and by the time we'd made the Chrysler V8 fit, the car would have become almost Corvette-sized.

None of those vehicles were proved to be financially viable, and the proposals faded away. With other studies, and the build up of personnel in the styling department, we were able to handle more elaborate colour schemes.

The Avenger had a whole new colour co-ordinated range of interiors, and the department grew to meet the needs of this. It was all getting too big for the Humber Road premises so planning began for a new site for design, product development, engineering,

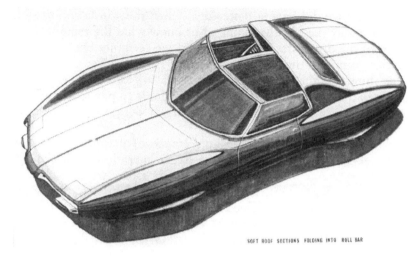

SOFT ROOF SECTIONS FOLDING INTO ROLL BAR

*Promising Tiger replacement model was dropped due to
lack of budget.*

and road testing. That really started to move on quickly in the late 1960s, when Chrysler International was able to put a bit of weight behind it all.

Big plans for what became the Whitley operation were hatched, with it becoming the base for European operations. But this was not all that clear to us at the time. The plan was to buy Whitley, an old wartime aircraft plant that built a bomber of that name, because it was close to Rootes in Coventry and was large enough to establish a good sized styling studio and to make a very good engineering operation and headquarters for Chrysler UK.

I became Director of Design when Ted retired, and on that day I remember Cyril Weighell calling me in and telling me about my new post. He said this is the situation, and this will be your salary, and so on and the salary he mentioned was pretty abysmal. I am not a person that would argue strongly with my employers about what they should pay me, but in this case if I was being asked to do this much bigger and more elaborate job then I felt the company should pay me for it.

Now having a feel for what sort of salaries they were earning in Detroit as well, that added a bit more weight to these feelings. I told Cyril this, and he was aghast, and did not know what to do about it. So he said he'd think about it. He came back and asked me if I wanted to make my case to Gilbert Hunt, who was then the MD. I said I would be very happy to do this, because he had made it clear from the start that he was a man with a strong feeling for style, and he believed that style and design sold products.

Cyril and I went to see Gilbert, and he said, 'Roy, I hear you're not very satisfied with the situation,' to which I said, 'I am not' and then explained why.

He said 'I think you're right and we'll have to do something better than that,' which he duly did, much to the amazement of Cyril. He told me on the way out that my salary was already higher than Ted White's; I was flabbergasted by this.

The amount of money we were talking about was very small in those days, but there was a principle. That made some improvement, at least until Chrysler International came on board, and we did have a better deal when the whole company became integrated. It was probably the fact that some of us knew what the remuneration was in the USA that allowed the dissatisfaction to linger as we certainly became competitive with other companies around in the UK in that period.

Another big thing was the introduction of car leasing for employees, and this enabled me for example to have a Rapier. It was very affordable to pay a nominal monthly sum, be able to have a new car, and one that I had largely designed myself; this was quite a boost and did a lot for the ego!

The period was also notable for the appearance of many visiting senior Chrysler people on the scene. The people who ran the R&D operations in Detroit, for example, these people were in charge of engineering, and were iconic within the company.

Harry Chesborough was one such example; he had strong views and sometimes made extraordinary remarks, or so it seemed to us. He and Elwood Engel were definitely opponents, and they didn't agree on much. The climate was not comfortable when they were around together. However, Harry was certainly charismatic, and went on to do other things in Europe.

This was a significant time because the Chrysler International operations began to take an active role in everyday matters, and it began to become clear as to what was going to happen. Chrysler International had a mandate to bring the three elements of the European operation together, England, Spain and France. This was quite a task considering the climate of the time, and the differences in cultures.

As I have already said, George Gibson was brought over to be in charge of the International operations. He was a strong man to run the operation, and there were good people with him like Don Foreman, who ended up eventually taking over from George.

Don was highly competent with a wonderful personality, who also never said negative things about anyone and made many excellent contributions.

George began to establish his influence across the three companies. We, in the UK, were exposed increasingly to Simca and Barreiros, and were wondering where it was all leading. Chrysler Europe headquarters was eventually moved to Whitley near Coventry, which was the location for the new Styling studios – initially for the UK but scaled so that it could handle European work.

Bob Anders took over the French studio and Claude Genest then worked for him, but it was a rather difficult time. I got the feeling that Bob was a virtual shoe-in for the Chrysler Europe job, which was looming on the horizon. Irv Ritchie was there as well, of course, but he wasn't a serious runner at all. There was a fair amount of frustration from the Americans who were running that end of the operation, and as time went on we got closer to the formation of Chrysler Europe, and the Chrysler UK studios came on stream at Whitley, but things were not going smoothly.

It really was a big surprise to me when they chose me as the Design Director for Europe. I was quite sure the job would go to an American, very possibly it could be a new face brought in from the USA, if Bob had not made the grade. There was no hint that the job would come my way ...

The new Chrysler Europe organisation became an amalgam of the Americans and Europeans from the three former independent companies. It was Marc Honore who was given the job of Product Planning Director for Europe, and as we were good friends, it stood us both in good stead.

As two Englishmen we were able to stand against some of the extremely strong engineering positions adopted by Harry Sheron (Director of Engineering). Harry was also English as well making it a three-man English situation in Product Development.

In addition Marc's parents were French and had come to England in the wool trade before WW2. Marc was bilingual, helping with Chrysler France's relations, which were to subsequently become difficult.

Our working relationship was a key element in Chrysler Europe, and my one regret was that when I later went to the USA, our working relationship was broken. It would have been a very interesting situation that could have evolved in my later career when I went into business on my own, if the working relationship had continued. Marc stayed with Chrysler in Europe, eventually moving to France after the sale of the company to Peugeot, where he had a frustrating time until his eventual retirement.

I think Gilbert Hunt had been having a severe struggle with the people in Detroit, and that prompted him to go. When the European operation was fully formed, it was Don Lander who became the MD of Chrysler UK. I never worked with him directly, as I was no longer a Chrysler UK employee, but worked closely with him at Whitley where Chrysler UK also had its head office, in a separate building.

This was all a very big change, and it was almost like being in a new company. At the time that the Chrysler European operations came into being, my personal situation improved considerably, because at that time, those Europeans who became the management of Chrysler Europe were put on the Swiss payroll as International employees and therefore our salaries were closer to US standards.

We also received various benefits, such as a company car and in addition, a couple of lease cars for senior people. The end result of all this was better conditions in one sense, but worse in another and by that I mean working with the French!

The French were a strong and independent thinking group; nothing wrong with that but we were all supposed to be in the same team!

The Chrysler UK studios at Humber Road continued to work on the 'C' car. The upscaled Avenger was designed to compete with the Ford Granada and Vauxhall Cresta, and was powered by an all-new V6 engine. The body was influenced by the work going on at Chrysler in the USA, where a new 'fuselage look' was being developed. Although this design allowed us more freedom, there were still restrictions. The small size of the wheels and tyres and the need for high ground clearance did not help the car one bit.

It progressed very quickly and was soon approved for production. This all happened just prior to the move to Chrysler Europe. Chrysler France had a similar sized car in the works, with three body designs developed initially, one from the Chrysler France (Simca) studio, one from Chrysler International studio in Detroit and one from the Italian design house Bertone. (Right)

The American design bore a strong

Bertone's Chrysler 180 proposal was rejected by Chrysler's management ...

resemblance to the German Opel and the Italian design to BMW, which Bertone was involved with at the time but the French design was more unique. The British Chrysler 180 was thrown into this competition rather forcibly as a more cost effective solution, and to much surprise from everyone and horror from the French, the 180 was chosen to be the new big car for Chrysler Europe.

... *as was Chrysler USA's.*

... *and Simca's.*

10

Chrysler Europe: 1967–1985

THE TRANSITION FROM CHRYSLER UK to Chrysler Europe was most marked initially on the product front. The UK was busy with the Chrysler 180, and a few other facelift products, such as the Imp and also the Alpine Tiger sports car. This brings to mind the fact that this was the first time I met Don Lander. He was dapper, very smart and with a penchant for sometimes looking a little sinister. When I first met him, he had a black overcoat, a black homburg hat, and as a marketing man coming to look at product in Europe, he certainly had a 'Secret Service' look about him.

Don had come over to look at the Tiger because it was becoming evident that this car needed marketing in the USA to bring up the volumes, but the American marketing department felt it didn't have enough pizzazz. Don, a Canadian, was sent over to see what could be done, and I hosted him in the old Humber Road studios, this being before we moved to Whitley.

He could do so little, as there was no money to make any bodywork changes, and in any case, the car was Ford powered and the ongoing Chrysler powered replacement project became stillborn, as there was no money left. Chrysler's fortunes in the USA were not good at that time either, as happened from time to time, and there were the usual Profit Improvement Plans (PIPs) taking place to cut costs going on.

To add pizzazz to the Tiger, Don came up with the big suggestion of stripes, very popular in the USA at the time. We tried a few different types, but the ones he settled on, which I always thought were pretty dire, were black and white ones that ran along the lower part of the body. I really disliked it, but there was nothing I could do, because at that time the issue was all about trying to sell cars in the USA, and it was deemed that the US marketing department knew all about their customers more than anyone else. So the stripes were added.

In the end, everything was amiable between us, and Don went away with an agreement to disagree on the aesthetics of the thing, but the Americans got their stripes!

When Chrysler Europe was announced, Bob and Irv Richey were returned to the Interior Studios in Detroit. When I later went to the USA, I

A coupé version of the Chrysler 180 was high on the agenda around the time of Chrysler Europe's creation.

'inherited' Bob and Irv as members of staff in Interior design. Meanwhile, Bob had left a disorientated studio behind him, and the French operation was moved over to a new studio in Poissy, on the outskirts of Paris. It was quite small, and run again by Claude.

It was difficult to know what they could do and to find a meaningful role was hard. Claude eventually retired and the studio was closed, and I ended up appointing the guy who was in charge of interiors there, John Soldano, as the colour and trim boss for Chrysler Europe. He was based in France, and yet he was part of the Chrysler Europe design set-up, and spent a great deal of his time in the UK. All of the other styling chiefs in my organisation were UK based, so Whitley was definitely the main studio. Chrysler's European operations eventually moved out of Switzerland and into Whitley as well.

Whitley ended up housing the styling studios, the engineering departments, Chrysler International, product development and the headquarters for Chrysler UK. After George Gibson returned to the USA, Don Forman took over as R&D boss.

That effectively set the scene for the next five years of my career, which was running the Chrysler Europe and ROW (Rest Of World) studios. I say ROW, because wherever a non-US sourced vehicle was produced, our studios had responsibility.

So, for example, in Australia, where a six-cylinder version of the Chrysler 180 was produced, that vehicle with its longer nose was designed in Whitley (in contradiction to a recent magazine article I saw). It was the same for the two-door Avenger developed originally for Brazil.

There is often a very close working relationship that develops between an in-house design department and the representatives of supplier companies to the industry, particularly if a supplier has designers of its own. These relationships can be a difficulty, as it was the custom for in house people to receive gifts and tickets to events as social offerings to enhance the relationships between companies.

R429 was a two-door coupé spin-off from the Chrysler Avenger. It would have been a direct rival for Ford's massively successful Capri.

The R429 project also lent itself nicely to a four-door version.

This got out of hand to the point where such things had to be declared, and most of these 'perks' were simply not allowed. The relationships themselves are of considerable importance though, and perhaps even more so today, where much basic work is done by suppliers many of who have excellent design departments of their own.

ICI, the chemicals company, had a division manufacturing vinyl sheeting. After WW2, car seat covering was usually in 'leatherette', an unforgiving but hardwearing material, except for luxury vehicles where leather was used. The leather then was without the coatings used later to protect from cracking and fading. Cloth was simply not durable but was used in really cheap cars.

ICI had developed a material called Ambla, which was a thicker and much softer plastic sheet that had some degree of stretch built in.

They were keen to find a market, and so a relationship developed with ICI to use the new product on Rootes cars. We worked with Frank Hoswell, who headed the ICI design team, and Barry Prince their sales representative to work out the surface colours and prints to give the material a leather like look and feel.

It was eventually produced with a perforated finish, which gave it a limited ability to 'breathe'. The working relationship with ICI on this product was very successful, but eventually leather became more readily available, and with new coatings overcame the wear issues. Buyers also became more affluent and were willing to pay extra. Fabrics also became more durable, and so vinyl was relegated to being used on non-contact surfaces in leather interiors where it was virtually undetectable, a situation that remains today.

Triplex, the automotive glass manufacturer in UK, was also very enthusiastic to work with car designers to produce better products and to help meet our goals. Anthony Clemenson was the marketing contact man for Triplex, and he was a frequent visitor to our studios. He visited competitors' studios too of course, and so he had to be very conscious of conflicts of interests, but he did the job well, and we had many successful solutions worked out between us.

A man called Keith Douglas, very well known in recent years as a motoring event commentator until his recent passing, was the marketing man for GKN, a company making many components for the car industry. Keith had been involved in the development of the now widely used alloy road wheels for cars. It was an all-new technology then, and the first application, I believe, was with Colin Chapman for his Lotus GP cars. Colin was always after weight savings. Keith thought there was a use for these wheels in passenger cars, and came to see me to talk it over.

This was in the Avenger design period and I was enthusiastic, seeing the potential for a great deal of flexibility in the design of such wheels. Until then the cheapest wheels for cars had a simple hubcap as a finisher, and more expensive models had a full wheel cover in bright finish. Later the Rostyle wheel in stamped steel was used on the Rapier H120, but alloy would in my view give us a revolutionary opportunity to break away with a huge potential for variety.

Keith was over the moon with this reaction and we worked together for many years on alloy wheels. Keith became a good friend and this was another example of a very productive working relationship with suppliers.

These relationships were creative, especially when the supplier had a design operation of their own to work with but many of the marketing personalities mentioned above had great enthusiasm to work with us to ensure a product being developed by their companies was directed in a way that we could find useful.

Of course we also visited suppliers in other countries in Europe too. I remember one visit to a company called Treves, which was similar to ICI in the UK as it manufactured Vinyl and textiles too. It was a family owned business and the company had plants in various locations in France.

Raymond Treves was the most senior man but had sort of semi retired by then but liked to visit the plants with me when they had something they wanted to show me. On one occasion I was taken to see their vinyl plant south of Lyon and my host was Bernard Treves the grandson of Raymond with Raymond coming along.

The plant was in an area of the Massif Central area of France and not easy to get to. We toured the plant and as we went around Raymond would greet each of the employees with a, 'Bonjour Claude' or 'Henri' or 'Gaston' and an enquiry as to how the family were. I was most impressed by this feat of memory and said so to Bernard who replied, 'Yes the workers love it, of course they are not the correct first names but it works nevertheless'!

It turned out to be an interesting, and sometimes frustrating, five years. My job required a great deal of travel between USA and into Europe between Spain, France, England, Germany and Italy. I would fly over to France once or often twice a week and frequently to Spain as well as many other destinations.

I spent a great deal of time away from home at this point in time. My wife was holding the fort very well but she was taking the brunt of looking after the children. I was often late home and away for periods of time, at a time when it was not easy to phone home.

Nowadays it's a regular and easy contact between someone in this kind of working situation and with communication with home either email and webcam or telephone is a piece of cake. In those days I would go to places where it was not even possible to telephone. I'd also find myself having to travel on to other places. I'd leave home on a Monday morning going to France, say, and I was not really sure where I would end up or when I would get home.

We had this arrangement at home where my wife would try not to worry about any of that. There would be little communication between us when I was away, she didn't always know where I was or when I'd be coming back and we just had to live with it. I remember it coming to a head one night when I came home, very late, and I had forgotten my key, I rang the doorbell and my wife came to the door, looked me in the eye and said, 'Yes?' Shows you how long I'd been away!

It brought things into focus, so I tried a little harder to communicate and work things out. Pat was very strong in running the household during that time and I am forever grateful to her for doing it.

George Gibson proved to be a good guy to work for, because he felt very strongly and told us very straightforwardly that this travelling around was no joke. It was no picnic and we would find it hard on ourselves and on our families and while we were away, we were not to feel we were to skimp on our accommodation for example.

We were always booked into the best hotels and we were always looked after well while we were on these trips and it was at least some degree of compensation for the lack of family life that existed during that time.

Mark and I, who travelled a great deal together found that a great comfort to both of us. It was nice to know that no one was saying, 'Well you're going on this trip and will stay in this cheap hotel and you must do this that and the other,' there was none of that so that was at least some compensation.

We were both on the Geneva payroll by then so at least remuneration

As the Chrysler 180 coupé programme developed, the money to get it into production started to run out. This model dates to 1972.

too was considerably better than it had been, maybe not up to American levels at that point but not far off, therefore we were all feeling much more comfortable and secure financially.

This was in the days when I had a company car all the time, even two or more, company cars that came with the job or were leased, so we always had good means of transport. Many cars were brought in for evaluation purposes too, so I would drive a different car almost every night.

This had its disadvantages, in fact, in later years I've enjoyed keeping a car for some time and consider it a luxury to keep it for five years or so, getting used to it and being comfortable with it rather than having to change a company car, in some cases as frequently as every three months.

Looking back on it, I feel this was not a good system to evaluate competitive vehicles because it was such a fleeting evaluation.

A 1972 saloon spin-off from the Chrysler 180 programme looked promising.

I had a wonderful opportunity to compare cars, many different ones, but with cars that take longer to appreciate the qualities of, such as Mercedes-Benz, a very fleeting exposure can leave you thinking, 'what is all this about?' when a longer term relationship with such a car makes you really warm to its qualities.

This 'one night stand' thing that we had with various cars was not necessarily all good and it could also be confusing.

Flying out of Heathrow on a regular basis, I would often drive down late at night, park the car and away I went in the plane and came back a day or so later and not remember where I had left the car!

Coupés were seen as a potential money-spinner, and yet none made it into production at Chrysler. A missed opportunity.

This came to a climax with me one time when I arrive at Heathrow and not only could I not remember where I'd left my car, I couldn't remember what I was driving!

I spent an hour or more tramping around various areas of the car park that I was familiar with and usually parked in, trying to find the vehicle and hoping something rang a bell to remind me what it was.

I did eventually recover the car, but after that I used to note down what the car was and where I'd left it, because the last thing you want late at night arriving at an airport is to not remember where you've put your car or what it is. Of course these cars were right hand drive and left hand drive, all kinds of different configurations.

There were also dramatic trips I had to take.

I can think of one in particular going down to Australia, flying there via San Francisco, Fiji and down to Adelaide, which is where Chrysler had its plant. I arrived there only to find there was a fax waiting for me saying 'you are needed back in the UK, please get on next plane and return'.

On that occasion I spent one night in Adelaide then turned around and flew all the way back again via Hong Kong the other way home. So it was a round the world trip for little more than half of a day in Australia, you can end up not knowing which way is up! I'm not a jet lag sufferer but boy, that sort of gets to you.

I flew economy this entire trip as the company was having one of its periodic tight spells, but the one saving grace was that it was in the very early days of the Boeing 747, and they were having great difficulty filling them up, so there were rows and rows of empty seats and at least I could lie down and get some sleep.

But that sort of journey is absolutely killing. Such were the trips we did to various places. There was Iran with the Peykan project, Australia and the United States quite frequently as well. That sort of frequency of trip increased more and more and that made domestic life very difficult. It was all nevertheless extremely exciting for me.

When we were going through the Chrysler UK phase and designing and setting up the new building over at Whitley, obviously we were going to need new people to staff the place. In the early stages in the Chrysler UK period the Royal College of Art was just starting to establish a course for automotive designers and Professor Micha Black and his able sidekick Frank Height initiated this.

These two gentlemen were involved in the Industrial Design School at the Royal College of Art and had the foresight to see that the car business, as far as designers were concerned, was starting to expand rapidly and therefore they had something to offer by establishing a course for car design.

They decided it would be a Masters Degree course, which meant that they could draw their raw material from design graduates in Industrial Design Schools both at the Royal College and around the country.

Their initial emphasis was heavily on the engineering side of things. It was a case of getting involved in this project and helping mould it into something that would be useful to us.

They really needed our involvement because they needed the finance for all this and we were eventually able, together with Ford, to get into the business of talking to the Royal College of Art and trying to influence the way in which the course was structured.

As far as we were concerned, the first year or so was not too successful in terms of the kind of graduate that was turned out. There was some argument as well about whether anyone was allowed to fail the Royal College of Art course which came as a bit of shock to me as I thought graduating from these courses was entirely on the merits of the person taking the course!

I was able to be of influence as was Ford; I think we were the two main companies involved at that time, and it was largely Uwe Bahnsen and myself who were putting up the sponsorships. We were able to get the course on track and closer to our needs after a year or two, which was then producing designers to our satisfaction. We could commit to hire a couple of graduates a year, that's all we could absorb, but it did give us a new intake of people or at least provide a place to draw on a new intake from.

Ford had more financial clout than us and perhaps, at first, creamed off the best people. The idea was that a company would sponsor a student, just as still happens today for the two-year course, and subject to a successful evaluation the student would join the company that sponsored him or her.

That worked very well for quite a while but in later years, when I was involved with these things during my time at Rover, this established system became a little bit more ragged. The students realised they could put themselves up for auction if they were very good and also companies who didn't sponsor students at all could come in and pick off these students who were willing to be auctioned off at the graduation show.

I felt very badly that we were sponsoring these students and our money was being wasted, it was going to competitors who were committing nothing.

It was becoming increasing difficult, as studios expanded as fast as they did, to work out exactly where trained people were going to come from. In fact we still continued to draw, to a limited extent from people who had been in art related jobs, industrial designers or whatever but these were fairly sparse pickings.

We also did pull in people still from the Rootes Training system before the Chrysler takeover. A

These were exciting times for the Whitley design studios.

notable example of this was Gordon Sked, who joined the group around then, and also Mike Moore who I mentioned earlier.

When we moved to Whitley, most of the old stalwarts at Coventry moved there too. These were Bob Saward, Curt Gwinn and Ron Wisdom. Bob and Curt were both involved more in the advanced design side at that point as we had the space to establish an advanced design studio as well as the regular studio. Lynn Helburg, our colour design man, moved to Whitley during the Chrysler UK phase, just as we were evolving into Chrysler Europe.

John Soldano, who was at Simca-Chrysler France, was eventually made the colour design man for the whole of the European operations, as Lynn Helburg left, interestingly, to start a restaurant in southern Portugal. His timing wasn't too good but his restaurant was very nice. We visited him on a vacation, and were very impressed with what he'd done, but soon after that, Portugal had its revolution and Lynn was obliged to leave the country in a hurry and leave his business behind, which was a very sad state of affairs.

Keith Cockle was a new designer to join us. I can't remember where he came from but it was not from the car industry, and he would leave the company after I moved to the USA, going into property development. He was a very capable guy and key in the C2 Development. Reg Myatt was another man that joined us at this time. He had been with us in Chrysler UK, had a dry sense of humour, and was a very amusing character. He was a good designer who had done a lot of industrial design type work before and among other areas of experience he had been in the pottery industry.

I had a lot of time for Reg but unfortunately he passed away some time ago. Geoff Matthews, who is still around today as an independent, was another designer who joined us, but only stayed a short time as he felt he wasn't advancing quickly enough. He went to Ogle, and eventually came back again, but ultimately left to go to Citroen in France and then, later on, formed his own consultancy.

When Ben Delphia returned to the USA, another American designer, Bob Eitchen, who came with Detroit's recommendation, replaced him. He was a very capable designer and brought his family over with him as did Ben, but he was extremely nervous of living overseas, and he really wasn't the right choice for the job.

It was a difficult situation and he was not so comfortable to be with as Ben Delphia. As the design team grew, the personnel problems became very time consuming, especially finding the right people for the right jobs, getting those round pegs to fit in the round holes, and those with management skills into managing. Very often I had to take a flier with people who did not have any history in the business. After all, someone took a flier on me!

It is very hard to remember everybody but another person who joined at that time but in very different circumstances, was Gerry McGovern. He was at school at the time and I was becoming a little uncomfortable with the design college people, because the graduates tended to have somewhat of the sameness about them in terms of what they were producing.

I suppose it's inevitable in that type of background, in fact I can level the same sort of criticism today with many of the younger people coming along. I decided I would like to try a parallel course to taking a student and putting them through the Royal College by taking a student who I felt had talent from school, and giving them a chance over a two year period and seeing how they compared.

Gerry McGovern came to us on an interview and he had an excellent portfolio of artwork but, unfortunately, no cars. So it was somewhat an act of faith hiring him and bringing him on board to give him the training in-house and see how he progressed.

He came along really strongly and at the end of his training period in house, we negotiated with the Royal College of Art for him to go down and have a much-shortened course over one year, rounding out and broadening his experience in that way. This was a first for the RCA, but they did similar things to this later on. Gerry obviously went on from there, and is well known in the industry today.

Fred Barratt, who had joined us at Rootes from Ford at Bob Saward's recommendation, came over to Whitley as the modelling manager. Bob Clair, like Fred, also from Ford, was his right hand man, and so we had a very strong modelling team.

Finding clay-modelling staff was difficult because it was a problem to find anybody who had sculpting experience. Most of the modellers' backgrounds were in pattern-making because making patterns in wood for metal parts and castings was a very skilled job, which could well be described as modelling. But it was in wood and not as flexible as clay.

Nevertheless, some people with this background were able to adapt to clay, and the methods used in clay and their experience with wood merged the two skills in a way, which was very effective. These people were mixed with others who came from a sculpting background, or an art training background in sculpture.

A problem was that most people that came from an art background really had aspir-ations to be designers. While some of them made the grade and made the transition, many did not, and it was not really ideal to have a modeller who was really uncomfortable with his position, and wanting to be something else.

Throughout all of this, I was learning my own skills of managing these people and giving them the inspiration that was needed. I was also keeping the thing on-line and on-track, and I had to front the operation to the personnel in the base company Chrysler UK, France and Spain as well as in Detroit.

There was a substantial change in the hierarchy in Detroit, when Lynn Townsend, the man who had masterminded the Chrysler Europe idea, retired. John Ricardo replaced him and John's second in command was Gene Cafiero, an all Italian-American team!

John Ricardo had something of a reputation because he had to stand up and deal with all the difficulties of Linwood, the Imp, and everything else. At that time, there was a government enquiry into the company's operating methods and into who was really in control, which was all very complex.

John had something of a reputation in the US for being bad tempered, and was immediately branded by the UK press as a real firebrand, who lost his cool at the least thing, and got really very irate and threw his weight around a great deal.

In truth, that was wrong; he got annoyed and I saw him really upset a number of times but in circumstances, where I would have been upset too!

They were situations where he was totally exasperated by what was happening either on the labour front or in the performance of his subordinates, and he would lose his temper, excusable to me!

The Americans had enormous difficulties understanding the British and French way of doing things. Harry Chesborough had been sent to France to run operations there and had 'gone native'. Bob Sinclair, an engineer who had gone over there from the USA, joined him and also went native. They became obstructive to what Chrysler wanted to do, and the home office in Detroit could not understand why they were not doing what they were ordered to and things became very fraught on occasion.

George Gibson left during this period, and after he left, Don Foreman, an engineer with similar status to Bob Sinclair, became the head-man in Product Development and my boss. Don took a lot of abuse from Bob Sinclair on many occasions, and it was an all time credit to him that he kept his cool, absolutely, throughout all of that. He was a very capable man and also a very straight individual, and he would absorb an awful lot of abuse to achieve what he wanted. I have had many good bosses since but never one better than Don.

In all the time I worked with him, I never ever heard him say a bad word about anybody. Don worked well with all of us, as well as the European team such as Roger Bresit the finance man, who was French, and Pepe Montez the Product chief in Spain. It was a good atmosphere within the operation with these people.

When Don returned to the USA some time later, he had been diagnosed with a brain tumour. This was around 1977, when I'd moved to the USA, and he died relatively young, a very sad ending to such an outstanding person. I would go and see him at his home as he faded away, and even days before he died, he would be asking me to look into this and that and he would have ideas, and 'would I see if they could work?'

He was well past that really, but was hanging in there, a remarkable and inspirational man.

Chrysler Europe forged ahead under this new hierarchy in the USA, and there were a number of new product development bosses. George Butts was one, who later became the vice president for quality under Lee Iacocca, surviving to retirement age, a quite remarkable achievement considering. He was a nice guy, too, but also a very political animal.

He had to stand in front of the British government, when it had its big enquiry into the so-called misdeeds of Chrysler in the UK, and I remember sitting in on this. Questions were going back and forth, and George was standing up and answering them. At one point, the chairman of the committee said, 'I think, Mr Butts, that you are the Mr Big we have been looking for all this time.'

This was quite hilarious to all of us there at the time, as George was far from big in stature. I think all of us struggled to keep a straight face. There were others too: 'Borny' Bornhauser was one we were fearful of. He had a very fierce manner, and it was only later in life that I came to realise how much these were just facades in many cases and that these people felt they needed to be like this.

Lord (Geoffrey) Rootes retained the chairmanship through the transition with Chrysler with great dignity, though I am sure that he would not have been too satisfied with that kind of relationship. I did not see him as someone who would be comfortable in the American way of doing things, as his father was.

Geoffrey was a very gentlemanly, kind man, and I last saw him some years ago at an SMMT dinner in London, a short time before he died. He came across to my table to have a few words, which was very nice of him to do. Later on, Lord Rootes stepped down and Gilbert Hunt became the Chairman.

With Gilbert Hunt in, Don Lander was moved over from the USA as MD. Don was a very affable character, very easy to talk to, and absolutely no problem to have a good discussion with, rather different to the initial impression he gave when he visited us to 'improve' the Tiger!

He was a very lively man, all over the place, and I think if you worked directly in his organization, which I didn't of course, then he was a particularly demanding boss to work for. I know that he frequently called people back from vacations, and I think it was just a demonstration of the power he held over them.

I remember one incident when Geoff Ellison, who was Don's sales director, came into my office and told me he was just about to go on vacation. He had got Don this time because he was going out to a property owned by his wife's family, and it was somewhere way north in the tundra in the Hudson's Bay area.

He went out there, and all was well. The place he was staying in was a log cabin affair, which didn't have a telephone or anything, so he thought he was well out of trouble. One day when he returned to the cabin, nailed to the door was a notice saying, 'Please call Don Lander immediately', signed the Royal Canadian Mounted Police. So the Mountie got his man and Geoff came all the way back to England.

I was in my office a few days after Geoff had gone on vacation and he walked in! I was very surprised, and I said, 'I thought you were supposed to be in Canada. What did Don want; what was the crisis?'

He said, 'Don asked me what the heck I was doing here, and I said, you called me back.' He added that Don's response was, 'Oh, that's all blown over now, that's no problem, and you can go back ... '

I also remember an executive being intercepted boarding a plane to go on vacation and having to return to base!

On one occasion, while we doing the Avenger, Don was holding forth to a group of his directors in my studio. We had a number of Avengers around in the showroom and also had a project we had in mind as a replacement for it.

Don was very gung-ho and was keen that this new project should fly, and that the company couldn't exist without it. He was convinced that he was going to get the finances from Detroit, come hell or high water.

Off he went to Detroit to sell the goods. Times were bad in the USA throughout this period, thanks to poor sales and substandard product quality. A week or so after Don came back from Detroit, it had become clear that he had not succeeded in obtaining funds in Detroit, and he announced to us that we couldn't have the project. We were all stood around in the same viewing area of the studio again with a number of Avengers lined up as before.

Don was pounding away at everyone: 'I've said it before and I'll say it again, there's a lot of life left in this product and we can sell it the way it is, we don't need a new product. I said that all along!'

This was amusing so long as you weren't in the direct line of fire! To emphasise every one of these points, he thumped the Avenger he was standing alongside pretty hard. After everyone had trooped out, I went back to the car and there was a long line of dents all down the length of the vehicle!

Travelling to new places was a big part of my job in these days.

I had to go out to Iran to take to take some drawings out there for the brothers who owned the Iranian car company Chrysler was in a Joint Venture with. I was there to show them what improvements could be done on the Hunter, or *Paykan* as it was called for the Iranian market.

The routine was that when our people arrived in Tehran we stayed in the anterooms, sometimes for several days before we were deigned an audience, then we went in and made our presentation, and we then returned back home to be told later what the outcome was.

Out I went, and on this particular occasion, the Iran Air flight passed through Russia, with a refuelling stop in Moscow. While I waited on the plane, two very large Russian ladies got on board and started walking down the aisle demanding to see everyone's passports.

I commented to the fellow next to me that this was a bit of an imposition, and I thought I did not need to show my passport, as we were not getting off.

These two delightful ladies got as far as two or three seats ahead of me, when a little altercation took place, and someone was obviously not giving the right answers to their questions.

These two very large ladies then grabbed the two guys who were sat in the seat a few rows ahead and they were hauled off the plane. At this point, I said to my seatmate that I didn't care what they wanted to see, and I would be willing to show anything, rather than be dragged off a plane in Moscow in the middle of the night. In fact, we took off without these two passengers, and I will never know what happened to them.

When we got to Iran, it was very late at night, and this was my first trip. I shared a taxi with someone else, and we roared off at very high speed, straight over a traffic light at red and then another. We then came to a third one, and something was coming the other way. There was a terrific squealing of tyres and swerving, but we managed to avoid a collision.

I turned and said to my companion, who had obviously been to Iran before, 'Gosh that was really something, we've been through three red lights!'

'Oh yes,' he said 'traffic lights are a fairly new innovation over here and people generally ignore them, particularly at night.'

I was deposited in my hotel, in the early hours of the morning and went to bed. It seemed very nice, and everything was okay, but I woke up in the middle of the night and heard this very strange sort of scratching noise.

I didn't know what it was and came to the conclusion lying in the dark that someone might have got into the room. That thought was a bit alarming, so I reached out and switched on the light, nobody was in the room but the floor was a seething mass of cock-roaches.

Of course, as the light went on, they all disappeared. Needless to say, I spent the rest of the night with the light on!

The next day, the only other hotel with a room available was the suite that Don Lander was staying in. So I moved into his suite for the night in order to escape the cock-roaches. Don was very magnanimous in offering the facilities of the room, and that was the kind of thing he did. He was a very good guy to be around, but my goodness, he was certainly quick on his feet, and he knew his way around the world.

Don continued running the Chrysler UK operation for some years, and despite his rather aggressive management style, he was successful at what he did. Don was a wonderful ideas man. One of those was to ship into Australia Chrysler Valiants into the

UK in the late '60s as range-toppers. They were very large V8 engined cars, about the size of a mid-size US vehicle, but far too big for British roads.

Don was quite convinced they were going to sell like hot cakes, but the truth was, they didn't sell at all. No one was very interested in having these cars on a retail basis, as they were real gas-guzzlers. A few of us were assigned these as company cars, and I had quite a number in succession. They were used for maybe four to six months at a time, handed back, and another one was dished out.

The frequency of the dishing-out increased, as the cars in stock got older. So I had quite a lot of experience of these enormous cars, and what they were like to drive in England.

Not bad in some ways, but this was an exercise that obviously shouldn't have happened. At that time, Don was not alone, and there were quite a few Americans who thought that these cars were saleable in England. After all, what was wrong with an American car? It could be sold in England.

There was little appreciation of the vast difference in scale and the way the cars behaved and handled, and this was a bad decision in terms of sales and marketing. For me, it was quite interesting because a number of us got to drive around in these behemoths – one of those mind-broadening experiences!

Don Lander was quite a character, and some of the stories I can tell about him perhaps shouldn't be told.

Don came to me one day and asked if I would produce a car for him. He wanted a special Avenger with one-off wheels and different coloured interior trim. I had had a similar car built for my wife, and she'd used it a lot and loved it.

Don wanted one produced for reasons not given, so we put together this package of what this car should be and presented it to Don, who approved it and the car was built. When completed, it was delivered to my office in the studios, and I let Don know it was ready.

The car was parked outside and the key hung on the peg, and nothing happened for a few days. After about a week I came into the office, and noticed that the car was gone. I assumed Don had sent for it and had it picked up. I called the modelling manager Fred Barratt, and asked him where the car was, wondering if Don had collected it.

He answered no he didn't know where it was. The key was still on the peg so someone had obviously removed this car, I just didn't know who ...

I checked everywhere, including the security gate, and no it had not been seen. I then concluded I would need to go and see Don and tell him that I'd lost his car. I walked into his office, and he said, 'Hi Roy what's the problem?' I said, 'Well, I don't know what the problem is. I have a rather embarrassing thing to tell you about the special car I had built for you as requested.'

He said, 'Yes, I remember that.' I said, 'Well, it's gone!' He said, 'What do you mean it's gone?' I said, 'I don't know where it is. The key was in the studio and it is still there, the car was outside, and no one I've talked to seems to know how or where it's gone.' Don looked at me for a few seconds before saying, 'Don't worry about it.' I said, 'What do you mean don't worry about it? Of course I'm worried a car's disappeared.' 'Don't worry,' he said, 'just forget about it'. I persevered for a little while, but Don was firm, 'Just forget it,' he said.

So, I walked out of his office, and I sort of forgot it, but I've often wondered to this day what happened to that car, and what the real story was!

Family problems were a big factor for Pat and I in the late 1960s and early '70s. My father died suddenly of cancer at 61. He'd never been a particularly well man, but he had been a very gentle and honest businessman who was respected by everyone who ever knew him.

He was dedicated to my mother, and I can honestly say that I never ever heard them have a serious argument. They were just together and totally dedicated to each other. My mother nursed my father through a few illnesses, but suddenly around the October–November time of his final year, he became seriously ill. Because of his various past problems, he didn't put any great level of importance to it. That was until he had to go to the doctor's because he was suffering from jaundice. He was immediately rushed into hospital for an exploratory operation. He was found to have totally inoperable liver cancer.

In those days there was no question of liver transplants, and so he was given three months to live. Three months later, he died and my mother never recovered from this tragedy. She lived with us for a few years, but elected not to go to the USA with us, even though that meant we worried about her when we left her behind.

She was in relatively good health, but shortly after that, she developed Alzheimer's disease, and after 12 years, she died.

At the same time, Pat's parents were very elderly, both in their late '80s, and very frail. Through this period, we had various family worries of that kind. These were the sorts of things that all families suffer, but at a time when work pressures were so high, it is difficult to cope with those things as well. I had to close my father's business, and various arrangements had to be made, which made life tough for a time. It was a good thing that these things happened at the age my wife and I were, because it is so much harder to cope with such complexities later in life.

11

Chrysler Europe – Product: 1970–1975

THE NEW FACILITY AT Whitley was a revelation. It was, at a guess, around six times the size of the studio we had moved from and it had in addition a large display showroom and outside viewing area. By the time we occupied the building, the Avenger project was coming to a close.

There was only the tidying up of the colour and trim programme and identity work for the final model line up. We were starting to look at the estate car that was to follow, and later the two-door which was originally designed for production in Brazil.

There was also something of a lull at this time because of the periodic shortage of funds. Our newly formed Advanced Studio led by Bob Saward, with Curt Gwinn assisting, did some rather fine new model concepts, the intent being to create excitement and stimulation for the other designers. Some very interesting interior design work came out of this studio too.

The C car (Chrysler 180), intended originally as a UK car, possibly to be badged a Humber, was also essentially completed when we moved to Whitley. Curt Gwinn and I led the exterior design, which was heavily influenced by the American parent company.

In retrospect, this was a further blow to keeping an individual British style, but the domestically owned companies were rather unsure of their direction at the time, and some poor design work was being done.

The exception was Jaguar, which retained a unique British feel, due to the direct involvement of the chairman, William Lyons, who had a real feel for the design of his cars. I think Sir William was a genius in the way that he evolved his designs keeping the 'Jaguar' feel through the years.

Though not a designer in the current sense, he had incredible flair, and despite many very capable people being involved in Jaguar design since his demise, no one has managed to find the real secret of 'Jaguarness'.

The Avenger estate and two-door went smoothly through the design process. These were strictly for Chrysler UK, so there were no complications with the French marketing group. We also investigated a coupé version of the Avenger, known as R429, to compete with the very successful Ford Capri.

Detroit was really waking up to the small car scene and had decided to market the Avenger there as a Plymouth Cricket. The coupé idea was of even more interest to them, and they considered manufacture of

R424 Sunbeam was developed using as much existing hardware as possible.

this car in the USA. The design worked well, maybe a bit too American for the European market, but so was the Capri.

We were all pleased with the design, and so were the Americans, but in the event investment funds, again, became hard to come by and the project was cancelled both for the UK and the USA. This was not the end of the idea of a coupé being designed in Europe for the American market, as I will relate later.

We also designed a four-door derivative of that car, showing how the front end of the coupé could be used to revitalise the Avenger shape, and also provide a successor to the then current Avenger saloon. There were also various coupé proposals on the Chrysler C body, and these too were also of considerable interest to the USA.

All of these coupé projects fell apart when the USA lost interest, or changed direction, and when the added volume for sales in the USA was taken away, they became unviable based on sales projections in Europe alone.

There were at least three C Coupés, one of which went to considerable lengths of feasibility, and was virtually ready to move into the production process. New four-doors were also developed from that project. These were quite large and involved programmes which went right through the design process and into finalised engineering. Like the R429 and variants, they were cancelled late in the day, all a colossal waste of time and money.

While it is not unusual in any design department to go through designs that are stillborn like that, this happened rather too many times, wasting far too much design and engineering time.

Eventually, Don Lander felt that he desperately needed a small car of some sort, and was pushing hard to get it. I suggested that we could do a short version using existing car components. This met the minimum finances available at that time, and is how the R424 (Sunbeam) was developed.

This design was effectively a shortened Horizon with a truncated rear, and a glass hatchback, mounted on a RWD Avenger floorpan. It was the last project I was involved with before moving to the USA.

It was a very short and focused programme, with everyone having to come to the party. Very strict controls imposed on the use of existing parts to control the costs, and the end result was more than satisfactory given the constraints. It was not the best car in the world, but it was a saleable product for Chrysler UK at a time when it was most needed.

The European project that followed the R424 was the C9 (Tagora) and that was entirely the responsibility Art Blakeslee, my successor as Design Director of Chrysler Europe.

The European projects were somewhat different.

The C6 (Alpine) was the first Anglo-French project designed as a European product that could be marketed in all European countries. It was decided to base the design on the Simca 1100 then produced in France. This was a front wheel drive car, and therefore something that Chrysler UK did not have. The Imp was, of course, a rear engined design, and for a whole raft of reasons it would be dropped.

C6 was effectively a long wheelbase version of the 1100, a car that had a good reputation in France and Spain, but which was considered to be a utilitarian shape by the British designers.

First thoughts of the C6 Project, which became the Chrysler Alpine, was this stretched version of the Simca 1100. This was clearly a saloon and hatch.

We thought it had an appeal to those who liked all things French! It performed well, was comfortable enough, and had good practicality with its hatchback rear. At the time, few Americans could understand it at all, considering it to be quirky!

None of this was a particular problem for us, as the package was basically fine, and we would be giving it an all-new body. The problem, if there was one, was that this was the first time we set about on a truly joint project between the French and British constituents of Chrysler Europe. Not only that, but the situation was complicated by the involvement of the Americans.

I should point out that Sales and Marketing together with Product Planning and other key functions, were all present in the three European companies and it was our job in Chrysler Europe to make sure everyone was on board the project.

There were many difficult situations with the French marketing and sales group, though the manufacturing group in France turned out to be supportive when it mattered. The era of flat panels, and what Bill Mitchell of GM described as the folded paper look, was in vogue but in the USA, panels were still very curvaceous.

We had produced our design with relatively flat surfaces, and had not encountered much problem from the French manufacturing people. We were quite astonished, then, when the Americans announced that these shapes were too flat, and that the company had standards for this. They told me that their expert on this subject would be coming over to inspect the clay model. He would bring his box of sweeps, (which are aluminium curves that can be laid on a surface,) and that if our design did not comply we would have to change it.

I had initially had some problem from our European manufacturing people regarding this, as flat panels were much more difficult to control in terms of surface quality. I had countered by buying an Audi 80, which was new then, and an excellent example of such a design with impeccable surface quality.

I brought over the head manufacturing man from France, Jean Peronin, and showed him our model alongside the Audi, expressing surprise that his people said it could not be done when we had a German car that showed that it could be done. He took the bait and assured me that he could do such things at least as well as the Germans, and so we were off and running.

When he heard that the American with the sweeps was coming over, he said: 'Don't worry I will send over two of my men to be with you when they come and it will be okay.'

The day arrived, and we all met with the American, who placed his sweeps on our clay and pronounced it impossible. The Frenchmen listened without a word, and when he was finished they made a very derogatory French gesture and told him he was full of something nasty (all in French) and walked away. The American packed his sweeps and returned to the USA, and we heard no more.

The French could be powerful helpers when they wanted to be!

The C6 was approved for production, and was introduced in 1975. It managed to capture the European Car Of The Year (COTY), and everyone at Chrysler Europe was reasonably happy. This car was a European product that could be sold across the continent.

The Alpine proved impressive enough to win the 1976 Car of The Year award.

It was very hard work to achieve a consensus in these early days of international co-operation, and looking back on this era, the real enemy was lack of build quality and poor corrosion protection. Many basically good cars had their reputations ruined by these two problems.

When looking at Chrysler Europe's performance in this regard, it was by no means the worst in Europe but the reputation, once gained, tended to stick. Of course, there were few Japanese cars around at that time but those that there were, were little better, because the move to high quality by Japan was to come later.

The development of the C2 (Horizon/Omni) then followed in the Chrysler Europe product plan.

The early stages of development in the UK and France were relatively smooth compared with the C6, as the C2

Initially, the 1100-based C2 project was benchmarked against the VW Golf.

was again essentially a re-body of the Simca 1100 and the French were already on board. Things were progressing smoothly, that is until the Americans came onto the scene again with their plans for the USA.

A sharper, mini-Alpine styling scheme was soon cooked up for C2.

Chrysler Europe was formed, as a technical group, under the direction of Don Foreman, but things were changing in the hierarchy of Chrysler UK. Don Lander was already involved with the C2 programme, as were the French, and then the Americans in Detroit became involved too.

It was a car that was going to fit into the range across Europe, as well as the USA in due course. The C2 was designed in Whitley, and the clay models were all virtually complete and awaiting final approval from Detroit, when we had a visit from some of the top people from the USA.

John Ricardo and Gene Cafiero were the two leaders in this group. These were very formidable visitors, and when they all arrived in the company Gulfstream, there was usually a viewing of clay models and final presentations of new projects for financial approval. There was a lot of interest shown in the C2 project, and there were a few who believed very strongly that this was a car that should be introduced in the USA.

There had already been activity in the US about the desirability of producing small cars, however, the big problem was that the buying public had little interest in them. They wanted ever-bigger cars and trucks, and any manufacturer that ignores what the public wants does so at their peril! Produce something the consumer does not want, and the product will not sell, and Chrysler had its fair share of this experience.

The high investment needed to produce a new vehicle remains pretty much the same regardless of the size, and small cars equal small profits.

This means manufacturers are very cautious when it comes to smaller cars. If they invest a lot of money into a small car that doesn't sell, then that will create a financial crisis.

On the other hand, if there is an unexpected surge in demand for small cars, they have to be ready. Chrysler was at an advantage because C2 was complete and in the pipeline, and the decision to manufacture it in the USA as well as in Europe was relatively simple. But there were development complications.

There we were in Europe with a design ready to go, but the plan now was to make an American and European version that was basically identical, but with some minor cosmetic bodywork differences to create an identity for each market.

Burt Bouwkamp was transferred to Chrysler Europe in January 1975. He had been the Director of Product Planning in Detroit, and was a very straightforward honest individual who says it how it is!

He was frequently in hot water for this back in Detroit, where he had been in the position of Product Planning Director. He'd been in the role quite some time, having taken over from George Gibson, when he came over to run the European R&D for Chrysler Europe.

C2 Short styling scheme from 1974 is a showcase for clean
Roy Axe design.

Final C2 clay model . . . without those extended
wheel arches.

Burt, therefore, took over from Don Foreman, was highly capable, well respected and was, despite the constant battles he found himself in, held in high regard by the people he worked for and with. While intransient at times when he was convinced he was right, he was usually found to be correct when the furore died down.

Before taking the role, Burt had only visited England a couple of times, and so he was fairly raw in European terms. As he was

Closer to completion, with the 'snow chain arches' now in place.

coming over to the UK, and was going to be my boss (I knew him quite well at that time having spent time with him in the USA), I suggested he came up to my home near Market Harborough and have dinner with us on the day he arrived.

I met him at the railway station and brought him back to the house, and as we were sat chatting in the dining room, Burt told us he had an extraordinary experience on the train travelling up from London. Everyone had been staring at him, and the reason was that he was wearing white shoes, something of a Detroit tradition.

In the late 1970s people in England did not walk around in white shoes! That made Burt a pretty obvious 'Yank' on British soil at that time, and he was curious to know why he was being looked at in the way that he was. He had a lot to learn in those early days but his good humour helped a lot.

Marc Honore and I always got on very well with Burt, and we still do. Burt and his wife Emme are still our very good friends today. He was very supportive of me when we worked alongside each other in Europe, which was not for long because he too could see that I was getting restless.

I was approaching 40, and was wondering where the Chrysler Europe position was going to take me. I have always had a feeling that, in the design world, ten years is about the right time to spend in one place. Design Directors need to change to free up the thinking in a company, and they need to be freed up from becoming too fixed in their ideas. I wanted to remain in design with the company, and yet I was at the top of the tree in my job there.

Burt felt that a move to the USA would be a good thing too, and as it happened, Dick Macadam, unbeknown to me, was having increasing problems with one of his directors, Colin Neal.

As I related earlier, Colin was the first American to come over to Rootes, while we were designing the Rapier, and was very supportive of me, while heading up the International Studio in Detroit before it was disbanded.

I spent time in that studio when I first went to the USA, and I always considered Colin a good friend and a strong supporter. He didn't interfere in our business at all, and was just a very helpful influence. Colin was running foul of the organization for one reason or another, but I think the chemistry between him and Dick Macadam wasn't too good either.

Colin had come to Chrysler from Ford, brought over by Elwood Engel to run interior design, and maybe he felt he should have inherited Elwood's job. He was also having big problems with Engineering, the relationship with Design and Engineering is always a prickly one.

A guy called Charlie Miles was really the key man in the engineering organization for interior design, and was very influential as a long time Chrysler engineer.

Charlie was a very flamboyant character and a really startling dresser, if I can put it that way. Colin and he were having serious clashes, and it was decided that Colin should be let go from the company completely all unbeknown to me of course.

But that created an opening for a Director of Interior Design in Detroit. There were quite a number of people around over there to fill that post, I am sure, but both Dick and Burt agreed that this was a position that I should be offered and so it came about. This all took place in 1975, a time when I was spending most of my time in the USA on the C2 project helping to support Curt Gwinn, who I had assigned there to liaise with the Americans, on site in Detroit.

The offer was made and I decided I would accept it and move to the USA. I did have a certain amount of trepidation, as Colin Neal was a man with a tremendous reputation, and I wasn't sure how I would fit into that organization. However, I knew all of his senior people the most senior being Tom Bingman, another person I would become very close to and rely on.

I have described the problems of a domestic nature at that time. Pat agreed that we should go, but was not totally happy about it. This was a big move for her, as she did not have the familiarity with the Americans I did. She had only visited Detroit once, too. The children were of an age when it was more difficult too but it was finally decided we would go.

Having decided to produce the C2 over there as well, the Americans had all the technical information, drawings and a fibreglass model shipped over to look at. All of this was done, and immediately, that awful thing, NIH (not invented here), came into play.

Most of the American engineers and designers felt that for one technical or visual reason or another, something was not right in the European product for the USA.

Inevitably, the whole design started to be re-examined and the first thing that was looked at in great depth was the front suspension. The Americans felt that the front suspension design was too expensive and too heavy, so they wanted a MacPherson strut set-up. As a result, they set about re-designing the front end of the car.

There were changes of that kind taking place all over the vehicle, as far as the design was concerned. Chrysler USA was one of the first companies to get into CAD at that time, and there was very little of that type of work taking place in Europe.

A man called Dana Waterman, a design feasibility engineer in the Detroit design office, was very enthusiastic about CAD and he had a good-sized department which was well equipped.

The first thing they wanted to do was get the surfacing of the car away from the

Unveiling the C2 prototype to Chrysler's European staff. The company was confident that a bright future lay ahead for it.

manual work that had been done in Europe, and put it into the CAD system. At the same time, Bill Brownlee, the director of design for small and medium car exteriors in the USA, decided that he was not satisfied at all with the shape of the car. It was too rounded, with too much plan shape for him.

This was in the days when the Americans strongly believed in the corner-to-corner theory: the direction was to make a car as long and wide as you could by stretching the design into the corners. That way the car looked as big as it possible, whereas the European direction tended to be of a more rounded plan shape, which you might say made the car looked smaller but sleeker.

Giugiaro's Volkswagen Golf was in the vanguard of this style trend and this influenced the Horizon. The interesting thing is that the Americans went even flatter with their panels on the later K Car, so flat they almost looked hollow!

The upshot of all this was that Bill Brownlee built another clay model of the C2 on which he modified all of our surfaces, flattening them and stretching out the corners, so that the car looked very square.

Some people thought this was a subtle change and why would we complain, but it was quite a retrograde step as far as we were concerned. Curt Gwinn was the man running that project with Keith Cockle.

Curt was the man I sent over to the USA to be virtually onsite, as all of this was done with frequent visits from me but both of us had our hands tied. We couldn't fight city hall, and if that's what they wanted to do, that's what they would do!

The car was squared up, the new front suspension for the USA car pushed the front wheels out widening the front track, and also the geometry of the wheel movement with chains and the Macpherson strut created the need for a very much wider wheel arch shape. The end result was a very ungainly shape with a large lip on it, which was necessary in order to get this envelope for the front wheel movement for the chain clearance rules.

The stiffer plan shape was then applied to the European model in the interests of commonality and that gave the European C2 an over-bodied look in relationship to the wheels with its greater plan shape.

There were a lot of changes, which just didn't come off very well at all. The product was somewhat bastardized by this sort of thing happening, which was all rather unfortunate. In the event though, a large number of Horizons were built, both in Europe and the USA it was a high-volume car, and the C2 also won the European Car of the Year Award in 1979.

Although this was supposed to be a totally common project, in the final products there were very few shared parts and yet to the untrained eye, they looked virtually identical. This was a case of a tremendous amount of extra tooling being required to produce the different versions of the vehicle, only to have them both looking alike with neither looking as good as it could have, which is the worst of all worlds.

In France, things had developed along, and Harry Cheseboro, who had moved to France to be the head of Chrysler France, was replaced by John Day. Bob Sinclair, who had been troublesome in his role of Engineering Director, eventually returned to the USA. Joe Farnham replaced him, monitoring the quality side for Chrysler International.

Joe had moved to France as the Engineering Director, and he had two men under him: Dave Logan, the chief body engineer (a naturalised American, born in Scotland), and Joe Mallus (who ran the road test and development side in the Engineering Department). These were three Americans who spoke fluent French, and that was a quality really hard to find. It was hard enough to find any Englishmen who spoke French, so to find Americans who did, was helpful.

Dave's French may have been a little strange regarding pronunciation, but he was able to communicate very effectively. All three were strong in the demanding French environment. Joe Farnham had a very nice corner office in Poissy overlooking the River Seine.

Joe and the other people running manufacturing and the marketing areas were also involved in product development, and we used to do evaluation road trips. It was a very carefully planned thing, flying down to Nice, driving cars back through France to Paris, with comparative cars along with the new designs.

Making the Horizon work in the USA wasn't entirely successful.

We did this on a few occasions, and it was very important to the French that they organised this trip very carefully with the right kind of overnight stops. This was all organised by the manufacturing director Jean Peronin and you can imagine what I'm going to say next – it was all very much a gourmet occasion, and really quite comfortable. I felt that a lot of the off-course enjoyment masked what we were really supposed to be doing: testing the cars. But the way it was organised, it was all very enjoyable and everyone looked forward to these trips.

But the big change was around the corner.

I was offered the position of Director of Interior Design for Chrysler in Detroit in the early part of 1976, to work alongside Dick Macadam. He was Vice President of Design in Detroit, where he had previously been in charge of exterior design for small and medium cars, and was very experienced, very thoughtful and conscientious.

Dick had succeeded Elwood Engel, and this was perhaps to the surprise of others there at the time, but I had worked well with him. I had often been with Dick, because during 1975 I'd been commuting regularly to Detroit, and we had both been involved on the Avenger and Chrysler 180 base derivatives.

I found that I was spending almost as much time in Detroit as I was in the UK, and Europe, and Dick was also trying to educate himself as to what was happening in Europe so he was coming over to the UK regularly. He was someone I travelled around a lot with while he was in Europe, and I respected him a great deal and we got on well together.

Quite clearly, my situation coincided with the need that Dick Macadam felt to replace Colin. So I was offered Colin's position, and he was let go from the company. I accepted the position knowing the prevailing situation, but Dick was confident that I would overcome that when I arrived. That remained to be seen, I had a lot of contact with the people in the interior design studio under Colin during my visits to the USA, and we had had plenty of time to discuss things on a business and social level, and this was a very major help.

Colin bore no grudge towards me that I could ever detect. Of course, I had nothing to do with what happened before I got to Detroit, but it was a potentially delicate situation. Our meetings since have been few, but have always been pleasant and friendly, a great credit to him I thought.

12

The Detroit Years: 1975–1981

I OFFICIALLY TOOK UP MY new position as Director of Interior Design in early 1976. Art Blakeslee was chosen to replace me in Europe.

He had also been in the International Studio in Detroit and had been chosen with no input from me, with Bob Eitchen, who had replaced Ben Delphia, remaining in place in Europe as his second in command.

Art and I knew each other fairly well and he had been running the advanced studio in Detroit up to that point, which interestingly was looking at Minivans in 1976. The chiefs in the Detroit Interior studios were Tom Bingman, who was the senior man, Bill Brathen, Bob Anders, and Dudley Smart who was in charge of the colour and trim.

They were having difficulties making the Minivan concept work because they were

Chrysler's Highland Park studios in Detroit.

Roy Axe with Tom Bingman working on interior design.

working on RWD platforms. Art brought over these ideas to Europe, where his new position allowed him to look at these products from the European standpoint too. The management in Europe did not proceed with such a project, even though there was one in the works, and Matra was involved. The Matra project eventually went to Renault, and resulted in the Espace.

When I arrived to take up my new position, alone because my family joined me later, Colin had already gone. I was relieved to find myself warmly welcomed into the new position. Tom Bingman, who was known as the 'Old Grouch', had already struck up a friendship with me and was very helpful.

I also struck up good relationships with the designers, who were talented, and were eager to move on from the previously uncomfortable situation. One of those in the design team was Michael Moore, who had joined Rootes working under me from the apprentice scheme, and he was a good man to have on the team. Also in the group was my old pal Gerry Piaskowski.

As explained briefly, the upset in Interiors was between Colin and Charlie Miles. Charlie was a larger than life individual, into very loud chequered jackets and trousers, and white shoes, the all-American image (by Europeans) of that time. There was a clash of egos, both thought they were right, and it had reached a total impasse. I thought that the priority was to repair the problem between Charlie and me (the interior department). I did know him before I moved in, but not very well, so I had the chance to really start from scratch.

The design group I was in charge of was first rate – it had the talent and ability, but had been caught up in this personality problem, and morale was low. It was suffering from almost too much direction, and was not working at all well. I needed Charlie as an ally, and as luck would have it, we got on very well.

I guess Charlie was ready to have someone in that position he could get on with, too, because the whole thing was reflecting badly on him.

I was really concerned that I would have problems coming in as an outsider, and by that I mean from another country. America, however, is a very special place; it's a country that exists through the merging of all kinds of races and people over a number of years, and another person on board from another culture was no real problem at all.

I felt then, and always have since, totally comfortable in the American working environment, but I did also feel that an external promotion might have been resented. But Tom and the others quickly reassured me that they were right behind my actions, and were delighted with the change that had previously been getting them down, they were all ready to go and I had their full support.

Because the relationship worked well from the word go, the transition was made in a jovial atmosphere, and the team was ready to proceed under a smoother operation. This meant that after six short months, the problem I had been sent over to resolve no longer existed. This was double quick time, and of course very lucky for me, things could have been *very* different if any of these relationships had not worked out.

After six months, everyone was feeling happy, and the operation was functioning as it should. Interiors were once again a force within Chrysler.

Support was excellent from areas outside design and engineering too. It made me feel a little bit of a fraud, as the basic problem seemed relatively easy to fix, it was purely relationships, but that's the way it goes, lucky generals, as they say …

In mid-1976, I came back to the UK to collect my family and move them to the USA. My wife, Pat, had only been on a couple of short visits to Detroit; Jane our daughter and Chris, our son, had never been to the USA, so things were very new for them. They all viewed the move with more concern than I did because I was already quite at home over there.

It was all an act of faith on their part, they went along because it was what I wanted to do and this was something I was very aware of.

One other difficulty was my mother, who had been widowed and completely disorientated by the loss of my father who died suddenly at the age of 61. My mother had lived with us in a separate part of the house, and had decided that she would stay in the UK. She decided that she would return to Scarborough, and so we managed to get her into a reasonable apartment there although the wrench of leaving her behind was very difficult.

We left our family Dachshund, Jasper, with her as he had heart problems, and couldn't go to the USA. It was a really a difficult parting. My mother subsequently only visited Detroit once, her first trip ever overseas and one she really enjoyed, before succumbing to Alzheimer's disease.

We sailed over on the QE2. The ship was quite new and I'd watched her being built on the Clyde on my visits to Paisley, near where the Imp was built. It was very interesting to have seen this wonderful ship put together and then to be able to sail on her to the USA. It was really an excellent experience, and one which we all enjoyed very much.

On the trip, my family found exposure to American eating habits to be rather eye opening – the idea of eating scrambled eggs and bacon with jelly and pancakes was not terribly British! We have since done many wonderful transatlantic sailings on the QE2, enjoying each occasion very much.

After a short and very eye opening stay in New York, we drove through the Adirondack Mountains back to Detroit. This was really a nice thing to do, the weather was beautiful, and it was an area I'd visited about a year previously with Marc Honore when we'd had a weekend off. I knew it was a good area to give the best possible impression before arriving in Detroit.

We settled in our hotel in the area known as Troy, which is north of the city, and a reasonably pleasant area. It would be home for a few weeks before we found a new house.

The initial problems at work were settling down quite nicely, so time was becoming available to do this and resolve the important and complex residency and legal issues.

Getting the children into school proved to be a good experience somewhat to our surprise. We put them in schools in Birmingham, north of Detroit. These schools were good in our opinion, as they also brought our two children, particularly Chris, our son, out of his shell. They encouraged students to speak out, be upfront and the system worked very well for them both.

We had considerable concern about the drug culture in the USA and we asked our children about it. They said, 'It's not a problem, of course it goes on but you're either part of it or you're not. If you're not, you stay out of it.' I have to say that, thank heavens, they stayed out of it, and we had no problems in that regard.

For better or worse, we'd arrived in Detroit, the job situation was settling down and we eventually found a house in Bloomfield Hills. It was in the area north of the plant, and not too far from the design office, although Chrysler was located quite a bit further south in those days. The company was based in Highland Park, a northern suburb of Detroit, on Woodward Avenue probably about 8–9 miles from the centre of the city.

Chrysler's offices and the studios were fairly new and sumptuous compared with what I was used to in England. The area was surrounded by largely black communities; and also alongside Highland Park was a Polish community *Hamtrammik*. This area was still very ethnic, full of Polish restaurants, and the like.

Interestingly all of that disappeared quite quickly and the next generation became fully integrated into the American scene and the separate Polish community no longer existed. It's interesting to speculate what would have happened in the USA if those communities had continued to exist as per the cultures of their original countries, as they have done in UK.

I suspect considerably more trouble would have arisen, but the strength of the USA is its integration of people and their keenness to adopt the American values and culture, a genuine melting pot, there are pressures on this now but it needs to continue.

Before I go on, a little history of Chrysler before I arrived is appropriate here.

The company had enjoyed a roller coaster ride of success, followed by near catastrophic failure. The company had a really strong period in the 1950s, when Virgil Exner styled the finned Chryslers. I well remember later talking to people at GM about this, Chuck Jordan, later Design VP for GM, said to me that they got the rumour that these new finned Chryslers were going to be introduced and they all piled into a car and went to where they knew these cars would be stored.

They peered through the fences to see these new Chryslers with these huge fins but otherwise quite simple in style. He said they were absolutely stunned by this and went back to GM scratching their heads to work out how they were going to produce some meaningful competition. Chrysler really did score a major success with those cars.

In 1961 things got a little stickier with a crisis over oil, and that was a time when the Americans all introduced smaller cars although they certainly weren't small by European standards.

The company introduced the Valiant, which was unusually styled, looking quite unlike anything else on the roads at the time. It certainly had appeal and it was the smallest car the company made for a long time. In the 1960s the first Dodge Charger came out and very big cars were very much in again, with the first muscle cars starting to appear.

In 1968, there was an all-new Charger that was used quite a lot in movies, *Dukes of Hazzard* being one example, and the car had a dramatic shape to it. The styling director for that Charger was Bill Brownlee, and I remember just how dramatic it was to drive, after being given one to use when on one of my Detroit visits.

Whether it went round corners or stopped was another matter! Many of these designs were winners, but were let down by poor quality, something that Chrysler consistently seemed to ignore.

In 1969, Elwood Engel joined the company as the Design VP. At first, he had to make the best of what he had. Following Virgil's departure, Elwood's own first designs eventually came out adopting what was called the fuselage style; they had an almost tubular look to them. 'Fuselage' was a good description. Those cars were really quite nice and in my early years there, they were my company cars, they were extremely comfortable and smooth, really nice vehicles in the American way which suited conditions at the time.

1970 brought the second generation Barracuda and the Challenger and these were very dramatic in performance and looks with their Hemi engines and dramatic graphics emphasising the shapes. These cars were cheap to buy too; today, there is a muscle car resurgence, and these cars are now fetching big money. These were exciting times because of the muscle cars and things went okay until the fuel crisis in 1973 and Chrysler had another rough time soon after that. Chrysler built these cars because that's what the public wanted, and at that time car companies could not sell small cars, there simply was no market.

It's a feather in Chrysler's cap that although it didn't have a car ready for when the fuel crisis struck, they did foresee the need.

Chrysler had been looking at its European operations for some time, and took the Avenger from England to market it as the Cricket in the USA. This was not a successful venture, as the quality of the car was not up to scratch. But many European and American manufacturers were producing poor quality cars during this period, and were simply unable to come to terms with quality and reliability and this goes for the USA (Mercedes-Benz, BMW, Audi and VW excepted).

Significantly, the Japanese had cottoned on to the fact that quality and reliability could be a major selling point. The lack of these two features was a major deterrent to buying cars, when potential customers could not rely on their vehicles.

The Japanese were putting a colossal amount of effort into building in consistent quality standards that would make them appealing in the market place.

They were also trying very hard to understand about the appeal of the appearance of cars marketed in the USA. Japanese cars before that era didn't look appealing to Americans, so they were on this double learning curve and the results were really rather dramatic. They also saw the poor reliability and quality of American and European cars, Germans excepted, as presenting the opportunity they needed to offer something new and attractive to long suffering car buyers.

Chrysler then moved on from the Cricket to the Horizon. It was something of a lifesaver, because they did then need that small car but unfortunately those same quality and reliability issues also continued to plague Chrysler, so there were pluses and minuses. Chrysler looked towards Europe for product but it's strange that GM never capitalised on their European operations in the same way.

Ford was also very reluctant to take British and German cars that were in production, and apply them to the US market. This was more NIH (not invented here) I guess! The C2 (Horizon) had its own problems, as it was not a Detroit product. It was redesigned to suit the market, a mistake in my view, and a huge waste of resources.

Another successful product was the Chrysler Cordoba in 1975. This was an attempt to introduce a low-cost (to produce and buy) coupé based on an existing floorpan. The inspired name of Cordoba had the connotations of Spain, and Ricardo Montalban was hired to do the advertising. His catchphrase was that the car was equipped with beautiful 'Corinthian leather', and with his wonderful accent it worked extremely well.

Everyone was so impressed with this Corinthian leather thing that it became a catch-phrase. In fact, there was no such thing as Corinthian leather, and it was purely a trumped up name by marketing, but it was a good example of something that worked. As a smaller car, the Cordoba was pitched as a Personal Coupé however it was a very large car by British standards, but it was nice.

On my visits to the USA I drove around in them quite often, and did a couple of long trips and they really were quite pleasant to be in, so long as there were only two of you.

In the mid 1970s, there was the tightening of emissions and safety regulations, such as impact resisting bumpers, seatbelt requirements, and airbags. There were also the infamous CAFE rulings on Corporate Average Fuel Economy towards 1978. Some these things were handled very badly at first and American cars had a clumsy look. Also in the mid 1970s, the VW Golf and Honda Accord started to make big waves in the market-place.

These cars were around when the C2 (Dodge Omni/Plymouth Horizon) were introduced in 1978 and the Chrysler product was no match for German and Japanese quality.

These were tough times again for Chrysler, and soon after I took up my new position, I had to think about the culture of American cars which was certainly something I had to make a transition into. There wasn't any point in designing a European car for the domestic market as such, nor did Chrysler marketing call for that. Subsequently, European cars have become much more acceptable in the USA more so than many American attempts to emulate them.

The public could not really grasp what these imports were and considered them little more than an amusing oddity. There were enthusiasts for such things, as there were for British cars a couple of decades earlier, but the vast majority of the market was still in, what I will call, the traditional full-sized cars.

To ridicule these cars from the European point of view is really being rather myopic. There was nothing about the scale and culture of the USA suggesting that small cars would become acceptable, but cost and fuel issues have changed all that during the next recession.

Jumping ahead to the period when small cars were forced upon the Americans in the 1980s, they never really did click, and it has taken until the 21st century for smaller cars to be accepted in the USA.

Mixed in with full-sized SUVs, there is a much wider variety of cars available today. It also has to be said that high quality cars such as Mercedes-Benz and BMW always have had an appeal to the wealthy, trendy buyer globally, and it remains that way today now joined by the Japanese premium brands such as Lexus, Infiniti and Acura.

All this is now in the air again, as the cost of oil has become so unstable, and a world financial crisis has thrown the industry into a downward spiral with no clear direction for the future. At least the US manufacturers seem to have woken up to the fact that they have suitable cars already designed in their European subsidiaries. But is it too late for them and can they be made profitably?

When I joined Chrysler in Detroit, things there were familiar. I'd been working on the C2 project for a year and America was not a strange place to me, so a cultural change to designing cars for the USA domestic market was not that great. I was well equipped and comfortable with my colleagues for a smooth transition. My family did have to learn, but the children learned quickly and settled into their new life.

It was the most difficult for my wife Pat. She had to learn to cope with driving, shopping and general changes in the pattern of life. There were differences in the product that had evolved in the USA compared to Europe. A typical 'mom's' car in the USA in the 1950s was the Suburban, which have latterly, or at least until the oil crisis of the late 2000s, enjoyed something of a resurgence.

In the early days, Suburbans were stark and utilitarian, and they fell out of favour, as, by the 1960s, did conventional estate cars, Then someone in the USA had the good idea of converting the commercial delivery van into a passenger-carrying vehicle. These were also used for the base of campers and still are today.

The difference between these vehicles and cars was that the suburbans and vans were truck chassis based, simple and rugged but not built for comfort. They had V8 engines and forward control, in the case of the vans. They offered a large interior, but the thing that really appealed was the driving position.

They were made in huge numbers but because they were derived from commercial vehicles, they were rather crude devices, not too sophisticated but were effective and very popular and best of all cheap and the interiors were well appointed and comfortable!

Because of the long wheelbase and large passenger compartment, they were often arranged so that there was a table in there as well. For long distance cruising, they were pretty neat things for family travel.

I had a couple at various times, and we did trips to Florida, about a 1700-mile trip each way, and they were just great for travelling with kids. The big saloons were excellent for long distances too, but they did mean children were confined to the (low) rear seat. Styling the interiors of these vans was an interesting challenge, and adapting them to passenger use was quite an exciting thing to do.

Of course, they eventually died a death, because they were large vehicles with a great thirst not good in a fuel crisis. That was essentially where the idea of the Minivan came from: something smaller, which had the attributes of the higher seating position, but was economical as well but more of that later ...

In the transition to smaller cars in the USA, FWD was adapted from European cars. The small American cars, such as the Chrysler K-Car, were very ungainly to European eyes and I had quite a bit of difficulty with them myself in terms of the design.

I was not responsible for exterior design, so I didn't have to grapple with that particular problem but the use of radically downsized American design themes did not fit well on the new package sizes.

It would have been a real problem to me had I been in charge of exteriors: the cars were designed completely parallel-sided in plan, the wheels were inboard, and there was an attempt to make them look as big as possible. The trick was to pull the corners out, making the thing very square in shape in all views, a process taken a stage further than even the C2.

The end result was an over-bodied looking vehicle, particularly so to European eyes. The K Cars were not all that bad to drive, they were satisfactory on American roads.

But there was this struggle the American management and marketing people had, as they could not make the leap from the traditional full-sized American cars into something so small. If the cars had more rounded styling, they would have been just too much to swallow. The end result was to make these cars look like small versions of the big cars.

GM and Ford had the same problem, and also had a struggle in those earlier stages. In fairness, Japanese small car manufacturers similarly struggled, but for different reasons, as they tried to make their products look like miniature American full-size cars. But in their case, quality and reliability started to carry the day.

Turning to personalities, Dick Macadam was very intense and dedicated. He'd succeeded Elwood Engel who was the epitome of the 'Stylist' era in the USA. An outwardly confident man, Elwood was not quite what he seemed to be.

He was not in tune with the radical change in the industry brought about by the oil crisis, whereas Dick was someone who understood the upheavals that were coming. Also and importantly, he understood the need to address the issues of quality and reliability, which the Japanese were making strides with.

Dick suffered great frustrations with his attempts to change the culture. New full-sized cars were coming through the design process, and they were destined to be dinosaurs. Nevertheless, Dick put in a tremendous effort to try to focus not only the design staff but also the engineering and manufacturing departments in order to concentrate on the achievement of quality.

It drove him crazy trying! He was banging his head against a brick wall. Ironically Chrysler had a close relationship with Mitsubishi at that time and they would have been, I am sure, only too willing to share their expertise in this area but like the Rover/Honda relationship much later, this was not acceptable.

'Not invented here' again won the day.

The old established companies were convinced that they knew best. I had a very good relationship with Dick Macadam, he was a man I admired for his consistency and dedication but as we will see, he was eventually swamped by the system.

John Ricardo was the chairman of the Chrysler Corporation when I went to work in Detroit, and I'd met him a number of times in Europe. I'd always found him to be an extremely nice person. It was interesting: just the other day, I was again reading a book by Lee Iacocca with a quotation about the time he was invited to join Chrysler by Ricardo. The company was in a lot of trouble, and John Ricardo was in need of a great deal of help, and had approached Iacocca.

Lee met with John, and he does makes the point in his book that John and his wife were two of the nicest people he'd ever met. I'd also found John Ricardo to be very much a gentleman, a very nice man but he had a difficult time coping with the Chrysler crisis.

Under him was Gene Cafiro, previously the manufacturing VP. That seems like an all-Italian line-up here, but Gene was very different. He was a rough tough stocky little guy who appeared very confident and ruthless in the way he would deal with his staff and really quite different in style to John Ricardo.

Intriguingly enough, it was John who had the reputation in the press (particularly in the UK) for being a firebrand. John was considered to be a man who lost his temper regularly, really quite an unpleasant sort of person as I related earlier and that was quite untrue.

Iacocca then went onto the open market, and a lot of people approached him to do things for them. He had a very good reputation in marketing and he was approached by a couple of Chrysler board members.

They had a chat with him, which led to a meeting with Ricardo, which, in turn, led to him being offered the position of President at Chrysler. His brief was simple: to sort out the Company.

We all thought that John told Lee that he would dispose of Gene Cafiro and I think he was probably only too pleased to do that, so he could install Iacocca in his place. Lee felt that the scenario being suggested was that he would become the President of Chrysler with John Ricardo as the Chairman.

John really intended to bow out, and he wanted to hand over the reins to Lee, as his health was suffering. Lee readily accepted the position, and he became the President and then the Chairman shortly after that.

A year before that, in 1977, another man, Hal Spurlich, left Ford, and he was something of a protégé of Iacocca's. As a product planner, he had been involved in many projects for Ford, from the Escort in Europe to many American projects and was something of a specialist in small cars.

He had fallen foul of the situation at Ford before Iacocca had left the company. Chrysler, who needed someone badly in the Product Development department, scooped him up. That meant Lee already had a man in Chrysler at the time he joined the company.

I guess the communication between them about the situation was not too good though, because Iacocca says that after he joined Chrysler he berated Spurlich for not telling him what a bad state Chrysler was in otherwise he would never have taken the job!

Hal became a very strong Product Development man at Chrysler. He was a fascinating guy to me, because in many ways he was an American with a very European outlook. He had very strong feelings about design, and was very strong in his leadership and that led to an almost immediate difficulty between himself and Dick Macadam, VP of Design.

I think that both of them were very sincere, they were trying very hard to do something for the company, and both of them were good guys in their jobs. But they didn't gel, and it was clear to us that things were uncomfortable. Something was going to have to give and it was not terribly difficult to work out what. But of course we did not know then about the Iacocca situation that was on the horizon.

It could quite easily have led to the demise of Spurlich in that situation, the old Chrysler brigade could have 'got' him, but in the event that never happened.

I was director of interior design, under Dick Macadam, and Bill Brownlee was my opposite number in small car exteriors. Cliff Voss was in charge of the larger car exteriors, and then there was Jack Withrow, an outstanding engineer in charge of the design engineering office.

This was a big engineering office, with us all reporting to Dick. The design office employed some 800 people in total at that time. Interestingly, Chrysler was experimenting heavily with CAD, and we were some of the first people in the industry to get seriously into this.

I don't mean computer aided styling, as this was something that came along much later. This was computer-aided engineering at the interface, with styling, where vehicle surfaces were digitized and converted into wireframe computer models and surfaces were developed from that.

This was pioneering work, and quite interesting for me to see how this was all done. Most of this was applied to the exterior of cars when I joined the company, and therefore I wasn't personally heavily involved, but I very quickly became involved as the technology spread throughout design.

These were very different programmes to the ones used in the car companies today, because they were really a development of the engineering computer software and were involved in the definition of surfaces of the car's body.

A man called Dana Waterman, an engineer at Chrysler, was attached to the design office to do this work, and he had a special area within the department to do it. Dana was very keen to press the use of these systems onto the design process, probably more than design wanted to use them!

It highlighted the difficulties where computers, engineers and designers merged together. In the early years, these initial engineering oriented systems were not always very helpful in styling cars.

But they were helpful in short-circuiting the long and laborious process of getting a design's shape from the clay model to an engineering and manufacturing reality.

What happened in the old days was that a car was designed in 2D then 3D, the clay model stage; then dimensions were taken off the clay model, and a drawing was made manually. This full-size drawing was the basis for the engineering requirement regarding the structure and the die model.

The die model was in pieces, sometimes called a cube, and each piece represented a panel on the body, and when assembled together this came out as a wooden model car which could be covered with Dynoc, a plastic sheet coating, which could then be painted making the wooden model a good representation of a real car.

Unfortunately, this gave the opportunity for the styling committee to review what was intended to be the final model for the design and make changes, not good for the accuracy of the model or the timing of the programme!

In fact, this model would often stray away from the original that was made in the design studio. The reasons for the changes were often for practical engineering requirements, although sometimes there was a little naughtiness that went on where changes were made largely for convenience rather than struggling to maintain the original intent.

All of this meant that when the management committee did finally see the real cars close to the end of the process, they were sometimes tempted to make changes yet again.

It was quite easy to make these changes on a wooden die model, the result of which meant that adjustments made on the spot with spoke-shaves and planes very often resulted in a model that was not representative of the drawings.

It does not take much imagination to realise how problems of fit and finish of the final product would arise, and in the USA, some pretty dramatic asymmetrical body dimensions occurred on vehicles leaving the production assembly line.

A major advantage of the computerised body engineering surfacing is that the original clay model could be digitised by taking points on the surface of the model by machine; these were converted into wireframe outlines then final surfaces developed from that, and once there was a good database on which to work downstream, changes could not be made without reference to it, at least that was the theory!

So, instead of redrawing a body shape a number of times after a number of departments had had a go at it, you had an original database to work from that could be referred back to.

This system is still in use today. What developed from that were numerous efforts by the computer people to produce systems the designers could use right from the beginning of the design process, to replace sketching.

But it's only in the last few years that any of those systems have really become practical working systems. I was involved with IBM and others to try and define what it was that the designer was looking for, how did he do that? Did he design with lines on a piece of paper like a draughtsman, or did he do it some other way?

The way I like to define it, is that a design is created in highlights and shadow. These things are much more difficult for a computer to simulate without reference points. In the early days of these design computers, many designers in total frustration turned back to the sketch system.

Even today with all the sophisticated systems that exist, it is still the designer's sketchpad that can often produce the desired result. Many people will say and I tend to be among those that you can easily spot a computer generated car design, because it lacks some degree of soul, something that makes it more alive, and more fluid.

You can see this in the development of the digital cartoon movies, because the modern trend towards electronically produced cartoons results in something that does not have the emotion and the soul that the hand drawn cartoons managed to achieve.

Maybe in the future it will, but right now, I do not think it does. That emotion is a thing that I think is lacking in some car designs today where the designers rely almost completely on their computers to produce the ideas.

The main engineering office at Chrysler was a very different thing; it was very powerful. I was lucky enough to know a number of influential engineers quite well, but many of these were also very opinionated. One has to remember that Walter P Chrysler himself was an engineer, and there was an engineering tradition in the company that carried on well after the post-war years.

Chrysler had its own institute for engineers and most of its key staff was educated there, and therefore there was a very big clique of engineers in place. I think that sometimes they thought they were almost invincible. That was a situation encouraged by the press, which often referred to Chrysler as 'The Engineering Company'.

It was supposedly engineering that was responsible for the reputation of the company. However, it was engineering that was almost proved responsible for its downfall.

Because of this total belief that they were the very best in the world, management was often blind to its own shortcomings! The end result was that Chrysler products became rather antiquated with regard to innovation, and poor quality became synonymous with its cars even though the appearance of the products had helped pull it out of the mire, two or three times.

That is not to say that the appearance of Chrysler products was always good because that was not the case either. This was tragic really as there was so much talent.

In case you are thinking that I have a complex regarding the engineers, this is not the case. A lot of the problem was that engineers and designers worked in separate boxes. It was my experience that if you put them together in the same environment and give them a project, they quickly understand the problems each face.

Very quickly, both parties get very creative and 'can do'. The formation of design engineering in Chrysler helped, but there was then still the barrier between that group and what can be referred to as the production engineer. Things are so much better now than 30 or more years ago, and I get satisfaction from the fact that I was part of the battle to change the system.

The same problem seemed to be a difficulty in GM and Ford too, and I am sorry to say that in my observations, it still exists in US carmakers. It still seems very difficult for the American 'Big Three' to totally grasp the advances the Japanese have made technically, and what needs to be done to put the same quality into their own products.

The Americans have yet to manage to apply that same level of competence, they are getting much closer but it may already be too late and a lot of 'baggage' is still being carried.

My first task in interior design at Chrysler HQ was to sort out the relationship with engineering, getting the team back on track with their confidence. All this before launching into the new designs for the new smaller cars, such as the C2, which was something of an echo of the European interior, but also the K Cars which were coming along, but needed all-new interiors. All this was taking place before the Iacocca era and before Hal Spurlich had joined the company.

As with the exterior design brief, the call by marketing was to produce something very American in appearance for the new small cars, something that would not alienate traditional buyers.

Therefore my hands were somewhat tied by the need to produce a smaller version of the traditional interior. We did try and present something more adventurous, but rarely was that totally successful.

Dick Macadam did put a lot of emphasis on trying to solve the quality problems, which he was very much on top of in terms of personal dedication. He became very frustrated at times, and would come into the studios if things weren't going in the right direction.

He would throw a 'Mac Attack' as the designers called it! Dick was very popular with the designers, however, who all felt he was a conscientious guy who was on their side.

The thing I had to get used to was the huge range of cars at Chrysler USA. They needed to be freshened on an almost biennual basis. In Europe these cycles could be eight-to-ten years, but in the USA they were only just coming off the back of an era where a car needed to be new almost every other year.

A major facelift in the late '70s was expected at least every three years, with a whole new car every four. That meant that with the wide range of product Chrysler produced the throughput of work was enormous.

Part of my responsibility was the colour range, which was very complex in the USA. There was a lot of emphasis on colour, trim and style, and the combinations available were just mind-blowing. A couple of years into my time there we really tried to work out, with the help of manufacturing, which of these combinations were ordered by customers in such small numbers that they were no longer contributing to profits, only to manufacturing complexity.

We did some research with marketing and found that the cars that appeared in the brochures as recommended to marketing by the design department as the most attractive, were by far the most popular seller in the range in the dealerships.

The combinations were carefully selected and attractively presented and were well accepted by the public too. We were able, by using that as a basis, to analyse these colour combinations and we were able to drastically reduce the sheer number of them. The favoured schemes were used in the brochures and dealers encouraged to use these combinations when ordering cars for stock.

This vastly reduced the complexity of the range. The result was to produce cars that the customer wanted and reduced the manufacturing costs and complexity, a win-win situation! In fact how manufacturing coped at all with all this complexity is beyond me.

Roy Axe helped refresh the Chrysler speedboat, and that in turn helped the Company dispose of its off-shore division.

Those were the challenges and for a couple of years I worked on these issues exclusively, and I was able to make good strides in many directions. I feel the interior group came together extremely well as a team and appreciation was shown at all levels of management. At the end of that period when we started to hit the really rough water of the (second) oil crisis in 1979, our department was getting very nicely straightened out and much more able to cope with the changes that came along.

I was able to visit suppliers' plants by sometimes flying down on a company plane, particularly to the textile suppliers in the Carolina area. Going down, seeing the manufacturing processes and seeing what they could do for us, in terms of design.

Another extremely interesting project we were given involved boats. Chrysler was the only carmaker around at the time that made boats, motors for boats, boat trailers, and the trucks that towed them.

The company was based in Plano Texas and I was asked if I would take on the task of doing something with these boats as they had a huge stockpile they couldn't sell.

Chrysler really wanted to dispose of the company but trying to dispose of it with such a huge stockpile of unattractive looking finished boats, was not working too well.

Tom Bingman and I decided that the basic hull and upper structure of the boats were not the problem and that some good strong cosmetic attention was what was needed. This was good news as we were very well placed to do this and costs involved would not be too great. There were several different designs of powerboat both with inboard and outboard motors, and there were also sailboats.

Most of them were small, but two were larger and were not included in our brief, the reason being that Gene Cafiero had given this project to his wife Nancy!

We set about developing a plan. The first priority was to produce something dramatic

'Little Red Truck' and matching speedboat really drew in the customers.

that could be used in marketing to show what was on offer. We realised that we could take this idea further and widen the exposure. As Chrysler made the whole kit of parts at the time we decided to take a small truck from the Dodge range and create a new look for it.

We chose the 'Little Red Truck', which was an attractive thing with separate fenders and narrow truck bed painted all red. We chose a dark blue theme and painted the truck in this basic colour with an attractive set of alloy wheels and a hood top (bonnet) decal in gold. A vertical chrome exhaust stack and tan interior trim completed the look.

We then added a trailer for the boat also in dark blue with matching wheels. We took the 21ft outboard powerboat hull, painted that the dark blue with a matching decal and interior trim. We completed the ensemble with a Chrysler outboard in blue with decals either side. It made a very attractive rig and could be shown at boat shows, truck shows and car shows. Quite a showstopper!

All the boats were sold quickly and the boat subsidiary was successfully sold too.

One amusing story worth relating: one day, Tom Bingman came to me and said, 'I need to do something about the work going on on the big sailboats.' These were those assigned to Nancy Cafiero, which had not caused us any concern up to that point. Nancy was doing a good job in our opinion.

Something had gone wrong and this time, we did not approve. Tom felt that I should intervene, very difficult when talking about the President's wife! We finally agreed that I should attempt to talk to Gene about this, something I definitely was not looking forward to.

I made the appointment to see him and walked across the expanse of cream carpet to his desk. Nancy had designed his office for him and had done a fine job.

Gene was very affable and after a few general words about the boat work, he asked me why I was there. With some trepidation I explained the brief, and that some of

Nancy's latest work had caused us concern. He asked what I had done about it and I said that I was hoping that he could talk to her about the problem.

His knuckles went white as he gripped the arms of his chair. 'I am not going to do that, no way, you must do it!' I had never seen him so upset all down to the thought of facing his wife over the issue. I expected him to go for me but he just wanted to be out of the loop on that one. 'You go and talk to her Roy, she will listen to you,' he said, and with even greater trepidation I did so.

'Oh dear,' said Nancy, 'I just had not realised, I'll change it at once.' It was as easy as that. I viewed Gene in a different light from then on.

Tom had also informed me that an excellent designer who came into design with Business Administration, Engineering and an Industrial design degree had been transferred to Product Planning for experience. This had happened before I went to Detroit. His name was Tom Gale, and he wanted to return to our operation. Could I make that happen?

The answer was yes I could, and after a bit of negotiating Tom Gale came into the interior design group. After I left Chrysler, Tom rose to the position of VP of Design and eventually after the Mercedes-Benz takeover, as Product Development VP. Interestingly, at the time he rejoined us, John Herlitz was also a chief designer in my Interiors team and later on I will relate how these two became the real stars of Chrysler design.

13

Detroit – The Iacocca Era: 1978–1981

IN EARLY NOVEMBER 1978, Lee Iacocca joined Chrysler just as things were really getting bad. He quickly became the Chairman and he was sorely needed. After his arrival there was a great brooming out of senior people, and a great sense of insecurity but at the same time a faith, rightly or wrongly, that someone was at the helm that would sort it out.

Lee worked night and day to get loan guarantees from the government to get the company going again and he succeeded as few others could have done.

One of the good things that Iacocca did was that he backed the Minivan project when he came on board. He also backed most other projects that were under development too. He could have thrown them out, and many chief executives who have been brought in would have done just that.

It would have been fatal to do that, as it would have put off the introduction of new models that were really not that far away from production, specifically the K Cars, the Minivan and others, and they were desperately needed. Iacocca embraced those projects, and they went ahead. The relationship he had with Hal Spurlich was a great thing because it meant he knew something about what was going on before he came into the company.

The big development was that Lee, to everyone's surprise, brought in a new man to the design department as a consultant. This was Don De La Rosa, who had been a design executive at Ford and responsible for the Ghia design studio in Italy among other things. Although he was based in the USA, that studio had reported to him, and turned out a number of working show cars.

Iacocca had a fascination for these small cars, although I felt that deep down his empathy was with the big ones. Don would receive these cars, shipped over from Ghia, take them round to Lee, often to his own home and there was obviously a strong rapport between the two on car design. Don, on leaving Ford, under strained circumstances, was out of work for some time before being brought into Chrysler.

He was located in Bill Brownlee's studio when Bill was in charge of small cars, developing the K Car as well as C2 derivatives.

Bill was smooth and dapper, and also with strong connections with the old Chrysler senior executives. He had been there a long time, and with a lot of good cars under his belt, including the last of the Dodge Chargers, no one can knock his body of work.

Don was placed in the corner of Bill's studio, and given a small team of modellers and was tinkering around with K Car sized vehicles, looking at them in a different way.

He'd come from Ford where there was a strong desire to move away from the sharp creased razor edged designs and designs were becoming more rounded. Don's brief was to take some of the designs that had been done at Chrysler and round off the corners and edges. This caused a lot of people to peer in at what was going on, and Bill to expound a little, in a not too complimentary way, on what Don was doing. But nobody was really sure what Don's position was.

There were grave suspicions at the time, of course, and you can see what's coming. Lee had brought in a few other Ford retirees like this. For example, Paul Bergmoser became the president of Chrysler because Ricardo retired and Lee had become the Chairman.

Before John Ricardo had gone, he had already fired Cafiro and Paul Bergmoser, who had been the purchasing director at Ford, was brought in to run the company on a day to day basis, as Lee was regularly commuting to Washington on the loan guarantees. Lee did, however, still involve himself in design selections and marketing decisions.

A host of new VPs were brought in, many with Ford connections, as Lee surrounded himself with people he felt comfortable with. To a degree, I can understand that approach, but it brought a great deal of discomfort and uncertainty with the way he was doing this. The old lines of influence that had been there for so long were all being broken down.

We were lucky in design in that Hal had come in a year earlier, so we were prepared for this and protected from the worst effects although we weren't prepared for Don De La Rosa. Clearly Hal was sceptical of De La Rosa, and was obviously not totally comfortable with it, but there was that connection with Lee.

Hal's own connection with Lee was quite interesting, because although he was almost a protégé, it wasn't a totally cosy relationship. There were a lot of disagreements, not all of them too visible to us. When it came to the survivors of the company at VP level, a

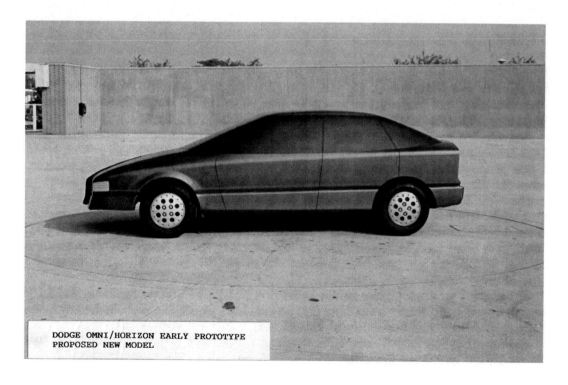

DODGE OMNI/HORIZON EARLY PROTOTYPE
PROPOSED NEW MODEL

CHRYSLER LE BARON 5DR PROTOTYPE

notable one was Dick Vining. He was an engineering man, but he'd become the VP of manufacturing, and was a stocky guy who liked to throw his weight around, a man to be treated with great respect, and not a little fear.

Nevertheless the greatest of people can be brought down to earth. I remember once Dick having a meeting in my office, before the Iacocca era, and we were all talking about a new product that was coming along. Dick was holding forth on something or other when the door opened, and in came my secretary, a very attractive lady called Betty.

She came in and gave Dick a message from someone, saying 'This is a message for you, Dick,' (she had known him for many years). As she was walking out, Dick said, 'Oh Betty, while you're here, just get me a coffee, would you.' She turned round and said, 'Well, now listen here, I am a secretary in this company to Mr Axe, I am not a waitress to you. So you can get your own goddam cup of coffee!' She then turned round and walked out.

The result was an absolutely amazed, jaw-dropped group around the table, but Dick just shrugged it off. It was something you just couldn't knock because she had right on her side and Betty could take care of herself.

Anyway, that was Dick Vining who, eventually came to a rather sticky end, so these things tend to go around in circles.

CHRYSLER LE BARON 5 DR EARLY PROTOTYPE

Going back to Don De La Rosa. His role was undefined, yet he had this team and the ear of Iacocca, and was held in suspicion by all of us. What was he doing? He had a designer assigned to him, who was not too senior, who was doing a lot of probing and questioning on Don's behalf, talking to people quietly in corners. It was all very uncomfortable.

None of us knew what was happening, but what we were sure of was what was coming. We wondered whether we should talk about this openly with Dick Macadam, should we assume that he knew what was going on but he wasn't always a man we could talk to like that, or should we assume he's a big boy and can look after himself can't he?

The upshot was that we didn't say anything to Dick and we all dealt with Don somewhat at arm's length. The whole thing was very unsettling and then one day there was an announcement made that Don De La Rosa was to become the VP of design for Chrysler and was replacing Dick. And that was it; Dick was out.

Dick was talked to by a number of very top people including Lee Iacocca, and was offered a very good and beneficial deal to help him find a new position somewhere – all of which he turned down flat and walked out. This was rather typical of Dick. This was just the sort of thing he would do on principle, and we were all very upset and worried about him.

He was out of the door, and we were all agog at what was about to happen next. It

DODGE DAYTONA BASED SPECIAL PROJECT

became obvious that we were going to see some big changes in the design office; just what De La Rosa had been up to behind the scenes, few people knew and everyone was waiting with bated breath to see what would happen.

In the event, the shoe was soon to fall, and Don acted very quickly. His first action was to fire Bill Brownlee, which didn't surprise us, because Bill had been quite open in his criticism of Don and after all they had been in the same studio for some time, and there was friction there. Cliff Voss, the other exterior design director, retired at that point. Nobody knew what the new organization was going to be, the power seemed to be with the junior designer who had been Don's ears and eyes for some period of time.

Lee Iacocca had made a General Patten type of speech to all the senior executives, which was a very impressive stage-managed affair. He socked it to the assembled crowd as hard as he could, explaining how desperate things were, and that a large number of heads were going to have to go. So downtrodden were the senior executives when Lee had finished his speech, everyone just stood up and gave him a standing ovation. Now there was a man giving the worst possible news to a group of executives, and he gets a standing ovation for it. That's charisma!

Don De La Rosa then announced a new organizational set-up. I was called into his office fully expecting to be the next one to go, only to be told that I was to be made the Director of Automotive Design, reporting to Don. I was the only survivor at Director level in the department, and in fact, this turned out to be a one-on-one appointment with respect to the design office creative staff not including the engineers. I was able to appoint the people I wanted to the senior design positions.

For exterior design, I chose Tom Gale and for interiors, John Herlitz. These were two people I had worked with for quite some time and who were my right hand men in the Interior Design department.

Tom Gale was a very talented young man and I have already described how he came back to the design department on Tom Bingman's recommendation. John Herlitz was a very talented designer and a good leader and I cannot speak too highly of these two, they were both honest and strong people and a great asset to the company.

Don was keen to get a new organization going and generally went along with whatever I recommended.

Hal knew things I didn't know about Don, and he told me privately that should I have any difficulties, the first person I must talk to must be him. The junior designer who had been doing all the cloak and dagger work on organization was brushed aside by Don and became a pariah in the department and no one seems to have heard from him since.

I knew all the staff well and was able to place square pegs in square holes with the invaluable help of John Herlitz and Tom Gale all with virtually no resistance from Don. We were quickly up and running and confidence was returning.

From the appointment of Don De La Rosa and Lee Iacocca, to the time I left Chrysler, the US car industry was learning to cope with the move to small cars, and the onslaught of the Japanese. European imports, while they were small in number, had the same quality problems as Detroit, and they too were under threat with the exception of the best Germans of course.

The Japanese had been making great strides. American cars had always been mechanically relatively reliable because they had large under-stressed engines, and they could go a long way on very little maintenance, but by the '70s, they were getting worse.

Chrysler had an advantage over the other manufacturers, in terms of product, but the company was in deep financial trouble. We had the FWD Horizon (C2) and before that the Plymouth Cricket (Avenger). The Horizon was appropriate for the marketplace we are talking about, but quality was just not competitive with the Japanese and Germans

The Horizon resulted in Chrysler having something people wanted to buy, unlike Ford and GM, which didn't exploit their European links. It was a small advantage, but it was all very difficult because of the financial situation the company was in. Lee Iacocca had to build on what was there. The Horizon/Omni was doing well, the K Cars were underway and the Minivan was on its way, too.

Don De La Rosa came in feeling that the days of origami cars were over. Many of the Japanese cars were more rounded and the car that really hit the market very effectively, the Honda Accord, was very well built. We took one into the studio for a closer look; it had a very acceptable shape that wasn't American or European, and it could be accepted as a neutral approach.

The only negative was that it had a rather small interior as the Japanese design did not take into account the American stature so some people found it simply too small inside. But the younger generation was embracing these Japanese cars, and they became hooked on the two things the Japanese had provided for them: quality and reliability.

They found that the car spent very little time in the shop, was reliable for long trips, and that it was sweet running, something that the Japanese had mastered in their four-cylinder engines, more so than the Europeans (BMW excepted). In contrast, American four-cylinder engines were pretty rough, and many still are, but why this should be so, I really can't answer.

PROTOTYPE COUPE

Chrysler was now starting on the next generation of cars, with a different philosophy than before. Gone was the shape of the boxy K Cars, a generation that I had a real problem with. Rather intriguingly the American designer, Art Blakeslee, who took over from me in Europe, was then responsible for the next car for Talbot, the Tagora. This design followed the Bill Brownlee philosophy of being absolutely square shaped. The Tagora did not succeed in the marketplace; it was a step too far, just as the opposition was turning away from the 'folded paper' look. To De La Rosa's credit, he recognised that too, and I too was very much of that mind, and so there was little argument that this was the direction we really needed to go.

We then embarked on designing the cars that were to become the new mid-range, such as the Le Baron. These were a little bigger than the K Cars, but quite similar in terms of their base structure and proportion but much more rounded, friendly looking and acceptable. There was also the Daytona Coupe, but none of those cars came to market during the time that I was still with Chrysler; they were designed when I was there, but launched afterwards.

That was the case with the Minivan too, but the design work was done under my jurisdiction. The position I held under De La Rosa was Director of Automotive Design. He also had the design engineering operations reporting to him as I said earlier.

I was not too aware of Don's background initially, although I became so quickly enough. He had taken an early retirement, shall we say, from Ford some time earlier but he was always someone who had worked with and related well to Iacocca. While the situation was not all bad, there were times it was very difficult.

We were moving towards more rounded car exteriors but at the same time we were searching for an interior with a softer shape too, because the K Cars were also extremely angular inside but it still needed to be American in character. The one thing that would have been a mistake at that time was to produce something that was a duplicate of a European car.

Chrysler's European manufactured cars at that time had no discernable American flavour, so we gave our new small cars a more USA friendly interior. The large cars were still being built, of course, and in fact the last one, which was designed under Dick Macadam, was the Imperial, a two-door with a Rolls-Royce style tail end.

A big play was made on the 'Ole' Blue Eyes' version, which was intended as a tribute to Frank Sinatra. The car came out during the Iacocca era, and Lee was a big friend of Mr Sinatra. The car was sold with a full set of Sinatra tapes and offered in light blue! These cars shared the same platform as the New Yorker, and while Dick had worked so hard and with such frustration to get this car to be better quality, in reality it came out as something of a catastrophe in that regard.

Things seemed to have gone backwards, but that was no fault of Dick's for trying; it was because the process downstream in the manufacturing areas had become worse and the quality was bad.

Eventually, the large cars were dropped, as they became passé and unsaleable. Chrysler's biggest cars were now the old mid-size RWD models previously known as the Le Baron, mildly facelifted and up-specced to become the New Yorker and Imperial. Both were dated but destined to remain in production for some time.

Hal told me about the difficulties that Don De La Rosa had at Ford, and there were people within my staff who also knew the situation.

Bob Eichen, who was in Europe with me, and Bill Dayton were senior designers who had worked at Ford and they knew Don. This background information was a concern to me, as I didn't know how I would relate to Don, but in the event, it ended up being a strangely affable situation.

He seemed to have quite a bit of trust in my position. I was the only remaining director from the original Chrysler design office, and was really left to get on and sort

Prototype K Car coupé was stylish in the extreme. It never made it to production.

out my own organizational situation. Tom Gayle, John Herlitz and I had worked closely together in interior design, and such was the strength of our relationship that it carried us through what were very difficult times.

Chrysler had always had a strong design team, with many loyal people. Many had been there a long time and they were a very talented bunch. They often produced work that could have helped to get Chrysler out of a hole had they been given the freedom to do it.

This was certainly no criticism of Dick Macadam, because in his era, he was receiving a great amount of 'help' from the senior executive management group who made final design decisions!

This group was dominated by engineering, and sales and marketing and these people had very fixed ideas. They were heavy handed on design, feeling there were ways certain things should be done, and therefore design had its hands tied to a great degree. Some of the people running the departments within design were playing along with this; they knew what was required to get 'their' design approved.

I felt that the designers had rarely been given the opportunity to show what they were really capable of and it was only in the production of show cars that their real talent had been visible. It was only later after I left, when new top people came in such as Bob Lutz who really championed design, that the design office was *really* given the opportunity to demonstrate what it was capable of.

Don had a very interesting managerial technique he'd picked up at Ford. He'd take three fine illustrators from the department, and would tell them the kind of thing he'd want them to do, such as putting a vinyl roof and the accoutrements of the previous era on to something like a K Car.

These ideas were illustrated very lavishly, and placed on an easel in his office. When senior management people dropped by to see him, these illustrations were there to catch their eye. He would know that these features would appeal enhanced by the quality of the illustrations!

Looking at some of the cars produced by Chrysler during the De La Rosa era, you'll see a number of them had this quasi-traditional look carrying over the features that we were all trying to get rid of. Ironic really, as Don was responsible for moving away from the 'folded paper' look while going back to an even earlier era for inspiration!

We were finding this difficult to cope with, but it was being done on one side, so it didn't get in our way too much when developing the all-new projects.

The Chrysler-Maserati was a product of that approach, where the later Le Baron convertible was illustrated with a Thunderbird type roof on it, even down to the circular opera windows in the quarter panels. It was produced by Maserati and was a complete sales disaster!

But there were a significant proportion of predominately American buyers that more traditional designs appealed to, and who would never buy Japanese. It took a long time for those people to come around, but time fades prejudices. These buyers related to Don's traditional ideas and they were targeted quite effectively.

Lee Iacocca introduces the Minivan, fully understanding the new model's huge significance on the market place.

EARLY PROTOTYPE OF CHRYSLER
MINI VAN INTERIOR AND EXTERIOR

It has to be said, though, that the automotive press did not react well to this approach. Tom, John and I were left relatively free to design the mid-range cars with Don's only input coming towards the end, just before the final presentations were made.

The Minivan was already complete, still angular but we managed to rework some of the K Car's angularity by rounding off some of the edges and smoothing some of the radii.

The car was really quite small on the road, with a footprint very little different from the K Car station wagon. It was also tiny compared with the commercial based products that had come before, but with a big interior relative to the exterior.

The real reason this car came to the fore so successfully was the move to FWD, which made this concept totally practical.

After the Chrysler Minivan had come out, Ford and GM followed with similar products, based on RWD (rear wheel drive) platforms. The packaging was such that they were really not very successful. It took Ford and GM some years to build a remotely competitive Minivan and many will agree that they never actually did!

The Chrysler design was undergoing development to improve the quality, but we didn't totally succeed in doing this. At no time did it come close to the quality of Japanese products. This was quite surprising considering we had quite close ties to Mitsubishi and I guess that's where 'Not Invented Here' comes in yet again because these products did not benefit from the lessons that could have been learned.

Speaking of the Mitsubishi relationship brings to mind an incident in the early Iacocca days. The Chairman of Mitsubishi, quite an elderly gentleman, was invited to come over to look at some of the new products being designed. These were displayed in the Styling dome exhibition area where all our new designs were presented. It was an excellent facility and all was laid out in a very attractive display to show the VIP visitor.

This was a routine used many times by Lee to show off the potential of the new designs to government officials and bankers. The Mitsubishi president arrived with his entourage, and was greeted by Mr Iacocca and his entourage. We set off touring the exhibits with a few others and me in attendance to explain things. The Chairman climbed in and out of a few cars, and lingered in one when we became aware that he had fallen asleep!

The Mitsubishi people explained that he had just travelled over from Japan and was obviously jetlagged. Mr Iacocca asked what we should do and they said 'better to wait until he wakes up'. With great patience Lee waited, and sure enough after a period of time the Chairman woke up and carried on as if nothing had happened! Lee knew how to handle such things and was not fazed one bit.

Don De La Rosa became more ragged as time passed, and he was clearly still suffering from the problems he'd had in the past. Drinking problems were not unusual in Detroit at the time, and although he was supposed to be on the wagon, he obviously wasn't. I found out in the starkest way, and that would account for some of his erratic behaviour that happened during this period of time. At least Hal was aware of this, and he had made it quite clear that if I had any major difficulties, I was to go to him, as a go-between for Don and Iacocca.

Don would sometimes demand the dismissal of someone invaluable in my operation, and this was done in a quite frightening way. He would come into my office, and he'd say, 'I want so-and-so out by midday', and no explanation would be forthcoming. He simply wanted me to fire the person concerned. I would then have to spend the rest of the day talking Don out of it.

It became very difficult to deal with this situation, and I found out later that this was often due to these people knowing something about Don from the past. Don could be quite paranoid about any threat to himself. He once told me over lunch, when he was in a mellow mood, that he wanted to give me some advice.

This was how to proceed in the business world he said, 'Just follow my rule, if you have anyone on your staff that you have any doubts about, even if you don't know what those reasons really are, just fire them. That's the best way of protecting your position.' That wasn't my way and I did not take the advice!

The difficulty with drinking would also explain why Don would come in very late some days obviously feeling under the weather, and this was at a time that I did not know he was drinking. He would be irrational, and unable to get with it at all. It came to a head, when presenting the new medium cars.

Don announced to me just two weeks before a major presentation to Lee Iacocca that he was going on vacation for two weeks. My response was, 'Don this is the critical time.' He said, 'Well you've been doing this, you can handle this, I don't need to be here, I'll be back in time for the presentation.'

I was very uncomfortable with this because, up to that point, Don had not been taking a lot of interest in the programme anyway. The models had been coming along according to plan, but there was more than one studio where these models were being developed where Don had never even set foot. Off he went on vacation and we worked up to our final presentation to Lee Iacocca of the models.

Don did not return from vacation on the day he said he would; he returned on the day of the presentation.

He didn't come in until late in the morning, about 9.30–10.00am. I went into his office straight away and told him he needed to come down to see the models as we had the presentation to Lee Iacocca at 2.00pm and he needed to see what these products were as he was not familiar with them.

'You need to make your recommendation as to what model you want to go with,' I said, 'I know what I want, but I really need to brief you.'

Don said, 'I know, I'll come down.' I kept pestering him every half hour or so, and he still wasn't showing any inclination to come out of his office, and I was getting quite edgy about the whole thing. This went on until 30 minutes before the presentation itself. I was busy getting everything prepared, lined up and sorted out but I realised that we were heading for some sort of catastrophe.

There was no way that Don could get his act together in the time we had left, not only to make his own preference of which design alternative he favoured, but also to be able to articulate the whole presentation to Lee Iacocca.

We got to the point just before the presentation and he said, 'Well, okay, let's go down into the studio.'

We went to the showroom, and I took him round the exhibits and told him what was happening and after a short while he said, 'Roy, I can't do this.' I said, 'What do you mean you can't do this?'

'I can't do this,' he said, 'you're going to have to do it. You make the presentation to Lee.' I would have done the majority of the presentation anyway, but Don would have had to have given the lead-in and made various pointers and recommendations, but the majority of it he had to be au fait with.

He said, 'You give the presentation from start to end, and I'll finish by saying that whatever you recommend, I back fully.'

I said: 'That's all very well, but you have to carry some can here and have input,' but he was resolute, 'No, I don't care, just do it that way. I'll back you 100 per cent.'

And so I walked into this very important presentation, which was a major affair and made the full presentation myself. A couple of times, Lee came over to me, which was quite interesting, and said, 'You're sure you're doing the right thing with this particular design?' (The one we were recommending).

I just got the feeling that Lee was not totally comfortable with making those judgements on small cars and by that, I mean cars in the middle range where there was not any sporting or other really outstanding quality to it. Therefore, he needed some reassurance, and I gave him that reassurance the best way I could, and he accepted it very well.

At the end Don said, 'Well Roy's given the presentation, and I agree with it 100 per cent.' And the recommendations went through.

The design was approved and away we went, but that was quite an unsettling experience, and I felt after that, that there was no way I could really trust those situations from then on, I had to be fully prepared myself, and well capable of handling the situation from start to finish.

My relationship with Hal Spurlich was very good, as it was with Lee Iacocca, at such times as I saw him, so that was at least helpful. So the working situation progressed and the overall feeling around Chrysler of course was becoming much more relaxed.

DODGE DAYTONA INTERIOR

The company was producing ideas, designs, and they were in the pipeline, and everyone was having the confidence to believe that things were coming right but it was not until the Minivan came out that things really came good and by that time I had left the company.

The Minivan hit an absolute jackpot and Chrysler was able to sell as many as they could make with the full mixture of options on them and that's always the full Shangri-la for any volume car manufacturer.

The profit margins were very handsome. This one product effectively paid off all of the loan guarantees, and allowed the company to get back on its feet again and ready for the next phase of its development. I really didn't have any major worries about how things were going product wise, and I certainly didn't feel under any threat for my situation, as Don had never given me any feelings in that direction at all but there was an uncomfortable feeling lurking in the background.

It was at that time that I was approached, out of the blue, from someone from my Rootes past, Harry Sheron, who was my opposite number in engineering when we were in Chrysler International.

Harry was someone I've always respected, even if we didn't always see eye to eye. By that time he was with BL in charge of the operations at Gaydon, a proving ground that was also the base for BL Technology. This operation was run by Spen King the 'Father' of the Range Rover, and was working on numerous advanced projects.

Harry came over to my house to visit us when he was on a trip to Detroit. He said:

'I've also come over with a message from some people you do not know called Harold Musgrove and Ray Horrocks at BL. They are looking for someone who can come over and re-establish a new design operation for BL. They would like you to go over to UK and meet with Harold to see if you'd be interested in doing anything like this.'

At the time I wasn't very interested, but in the back of my mind, there were some problems that existed back at home. These were my mother, who was suffering from Alzheimer's disease, a situation giving us some concern; plus my wife's parents' health, too, was not good. Then there was the situation with Don at Chrysler, which was making me increasingly uncomfortable.

So, this was at least something that prompted me to spend a little time thinking about what Harry was talking about. But I told him at that time that I was not really very interested.

A little later on another visit, Harry repeated the request from Harold Musgrove and he was quite persuasive about it. I said: 'I wouldn't feel comfortable for BL to pay for my trip to talk about something that I wasn't all that interested in doing but as I am coming over soon to see my mother, I would be quite happy, if Harold was available at the end of that trip, to talk to him in London.'

Harry went off and duly got back to me saying that this would be fine. So I went over to England as planned, in what were very difficult times there. Margaret Thatcher had vowed to break the union stranglehold over BL and the Red Robbo union thing was in full flight, but she was quite determined that this would be sorted out.

It was a do-or-die situation. I wasn't too clear about the 'die' thing, but certainly felt that there was some hope there but again, I really wasn't really that interested.

Then I had my chat with Harold who, much to my surprise, I got on very well with. I had never met him before, but he is a good 'Brummie', if I can put it that way.

He was a guy who spoke very good sense and didn't mince his words as he explained the situation at BL, what was wrong, and what was right, and what he wanted to put right.

He told me that the company was in very fine shape regarding manufacturing. They had this confrontation with the workers, but the manufacturing division was going to have a lot of money poured into it. Manufacturing was to be computerised, and robotized at the plants, and new models were in the pipeline, and all these things were going to be done.

However, he was not satisfied overall, he felt the weakness in the operation was styling (design). He also put great emphasis on the newly emerging partnership that was developing between the company and Honda, which was something I knew little about, but which was of great interest.

David Bache was in charge of styling at BL and although I knew him, I'd not been in contact for some time, and I had no idea what was really happening in the operation. But Harold was very persuasive, he said that if I were interested in heading up and revitalising the operation, he would back it 100 per cent, with money for new facilities, and other things to make it all work.

With this idea planted in my mind, and after gaining a great deal of respect for Harold, which has never gone away since, I came back and discussed all this with my wife. We came to the conclusion that with the situation at Chrysler straightening out, but with Don preying on my mind, our parents' difficulties, and so on, that maybe I should consider this offer.

To cut a long story short, we decided that what I should do was to go and talk again, this time at BL's expense to try and see if something could be worked out. Basically the die was cast at that second interview, and this led to me taking a position at Rover and leaving Chrysler with considerable regret.

I had actually worked for Chrysler for no less than 27 years (including my time at Rootes) and I had my 25-year service pin.

I admit, however, that through this period it felt like working for three separate companies, Rootes, Chrysler International then Chrysler USA. I had a lot of positive feeling for Chrysler and a lot of empathy with it, I liked working in the USA and I was reluctant to make the move but then I felt, here was an opportunity to set-up yet again another new design department almost from scratch, little did I know how much from scratch!

Therefore we made the decision that should something be worked out that would be acceptable to me, we would make that move. A deal was worked out that allowed me to keep my connections with the USA, and be employed in such a way that I could do this. Then I needed to hand my notice in to Chrysler, mindful that Hal had always told me that if things got intolerable as far as Don was concerned I was to talk to him first.

He said it in such a way that I thought I should tackle things that way, it wasn't a question of bargaining for a position to stay at Chrysler; I had decided to do what I was going to do. It was just a question of letting Hal know, which I duly did. Hal told me to go home and stay there, and he would decide how to handle things. He said he would then call me in to decide how to proceed from there.

He then saw Don, and what happened behind the scenes I don't know, but when eventually I came in front of Don, he expressed his disappointment that I hadn't talked to him, which was fair enough. At the same time, the meeting was not difficult and I was offered something very tempting to stay, but I made it clear that I'd made my decision.

After a series of interviews with various top people that was all accepted, and I was told that they understood that things were difficult at BL and they were not sure what I'd find there, but if I was to find the situation untenable in the early stages, I was welcome to move back, though not in the same position of course.

We therefore parted on good terms. In meetings I've had since with Chrysler people, it has always been on a very affable basis, there were no bad feelings, nothing that has ever made me feel uncomfortable.

14

The UK and Austin Rover Group: 1982–1984

DULY AT THE END of 1981, we packed up our bags again and returned to the UK. My daughter, Jane, remained in the USA because she was at college, and my son came to the UK with us.

He hadn't quite finished his high school and in order to get his diploma from the USA, they had arranged for him to complete his studies at a USA Air Force base near Oxford. That was quite ironic, as the studies he needed to complete were in American history!

We moved to a hotel in Banbury and there we stayed until we found a house. It was a traumatic move to a degree, the relocation being given the codename 'Project Jasper' by the Personnel department, because we shipped ourselves back and had to ship back our Dachshund, Jasper 2, who we had bought in the USA. He had to be shipped back and put into quarantine, a source of some amusement to the company.

We settled in to our hotel, and I went off on my first working day to the plant at Canley, which was where Harold Musgrove had his head offices. During my interviews, I had talked to Ray Horrocks as well, but he left the scene not too long after that. He wasn't too evident in the operation and Michael Edwards had also left the scene, I only met him once.

Harold was the man I related to, and so on that first morning in, it was a question of being shown the premises, which came as an almighty shock. You could say that I should have looked before I joined, but it's very difficult to do that with design departments; you can't really be given a tour before joining the company for obvious reasons.

The shock was much greater than expected, I didn't expect too much at that stage but it was bad. The challenge was to create a new department in a new environment. I resisted the temptation to go back to Detroit at that stage, though I seriously thought about it! I stayed where I was and after being introduced to the key people in the

The Roy Axe studios in Canley were a massive step forward from what came before at Longbridge.

operation, I was then shown by Harold and his fellow directors, a product that was just about to be introduced, the Maestro.

That exposure really had me concerned about what was going to happen within the company, but the die was cast then. My new career at Rover had started, and at least it was to provide some great challenges and with a good relationship developing between Harold Musgrove and myself, it eventually led to something even more different than I expected.

I joined BL at the beginning of 1982, and in a winter that year in England that was even worse than that in Detroit!

Harold Musgrove was a man on a mission to put BL back into the international automotive business, and he felt confident that he knew what was needed to achieve those goals.

I have had a career setting up styling operations and handing over the results to others and, in fact, I had gone over to Detroit on just such an assignment there to re-establish the interior design studio. This was another challenge of the same kind but on first impressions, it seemed to be my greatest one yet.

Harold felt that the manufacturing operations at BL were capable of anything given good styling and engineering. CAD/CAM was very much on the horizon, and a colleague from my previous life at Chrysler Europe, Joe Farnham, was already in place as the Director of Engineering.

I knew that the situation was bad and that radical changes would be required quickly but I trusted my impression of Harold Musgrove as a man of his word, when he said I could totally rely on his backing to support what needed to be done including the establishment of a new studio at Canley in Coventry.

I knew that things were likely to be basic at the company as regards working facilities but I was not prepared for just how basic it was. On arrival I was shown to my office, introduced to my new secretary, Maureen Hill, and to two old colleagues from earlier days at Chrysler Europe. These were Rex Fleming who had been someone I had worked with since my Rootes days and Gordon Sked, who I had hired at Chrysler UK, but who had moved on to Leyland some time earlier.

These two were the people who gave me my introduction to the BL styling operation. They were very supportive and were to prove to be reliable and loyal throughout.

Equipment was best described as rudimentary, and there was no showroom at Canley. This was in fact at the second facility located at the Longbridge plant some 20–30 miles away in a place called the Elephant House. This was a circular building with space for designers and modellers on the perimeter and a central area that could be used for display and presentations.

It was all in poor shape and quite awful. I was stunned and really wondered what I had got myself into!

I began to wonder what might happen if Harold did not prove to be a man of his word, but this fear proved groundless. In fact, the planning of the new facilities was put into effect almost immediately with special urgency required as the partnership with Honda was reaching a stage where a joint development programme with Honda's design department was just about to begin and the situation looked very difficult in light of the inadequate facilities at the company.

In the event, as much work as could be incorporated at Canley was done there, including most of the design work on the Rover/Honda project, while Longbridge was

Roy Axe settles in at Austin Rover – but it wasn't an easy ride.

used to service the other already existing projects.

The new facility was planned out and the cost thought to be excessive. I did remind Harold of his commitment to me and he honoured it as with everything else he promised. There was also strong support from the Finance Director Bob Neville. It is always a pleasant surprise and unusual for design departments to get enthusiastic support from finance departments, but it is always appreciated when it happens!

There followed over a year of very high-level activity. A new studio complex was designed adjacent to and incorporating the smaller original Canley facility. The new premises were inside the existing Triumph assembly building, which reduced costs. The studios were of good proportion and included good storage and display facilities.

At the same time the relationship between Honda Design and our operation was in full swing, with the early work of the Rover 800 project being done in the middle of this mess. In addition to all of this, the current products required attention.

An excellent relationship between Mr Iwakura, the Honda design chief, and myself developed in these early days, and that led to a friendship lasting for many years. As a result, the atmosphere between the two design groups was positive and worked well throughout the period we worked together, more of this later.

The second thing that I had to cope with was that on the second day at the new job I was exposed to the Maestro. I thought this design was a disaster (another understatement!)

The proportions were bad and the detail awful and clumsy. The concave sides made the design look weak and the whole thing looked totally dated. It was explained to me that the design was done before the Metro and that this was why the design looked old. This was only part of the problem. The interior was very poor with a fascia/instrument panel that, out of the car, had the structural integrity of something from a fishmonger's slab.

I was told that there was nothing I could do as the design was headed for production later in the year. I did try to improve the form of the front wing, which looked as if it was falling off the car but within the constraints of the tooling and surrounding metal it proved impossible, and I had to accept that this vehicle was going to hit the market like that.

The next day I was shown the Montego. I was stood in front of it and told that this model was over a year away, and so I had a great opportunity to improve it if I felt it was needed! It is hard to know what to say in circumstances like this, but my first remarks were that the design should be scrapped and the whole thing done again.

This was not acceptable, as the plan was well in place, but there was room to 'tweek' the design. The changes were really minimal, as the doors, which were common to the Maestro, had to stay as had the basic form dictated by the structure. I was able to improve the front and get rid of the Maestro look, and make some improvements to the rear.

By applying, admittedly rather crude, mouldings to the waistline, I was able to minimise the falling look in this area. The result was far from anything I am proud of but was the best I could do, this plus the chance to replace the fascia/instrument panel with a new one, which could then be applied to the Maestro at a later date.

The work on the existing products was re-evaluated, and brought under control and we had already started work on the XX project with Honda, which eventually became the Rover 800. Projects beyond the XX were also in discussion for a new product plan.

After considering this scenario I felt that there were two major priorities: the first was to complete the new design premises at Canley as soon as possible, and then find a new design team to staff it. This, of course, would take time and a great deal of planning, and involved moving out of Longbridge as soon as possible. In the event this goal was accomplished in record time. In 1983 we were able to progressively move into the new studios, which while no architectural gem (it was built inside the old Triumph plant) it was a good practical layout and proved very workable for many years.

Staffing this facility was something I was more concerned with. There were few people of the right calibre on the market and we needed quite a lot more people!

It would be very difficult, we knew, to get good people to join the company with its track record at that time. I had kept as many people as possible from the original staff in order to evaluate them and it has always been my policy to try to build on talent in place rather than just bring in new.

I had a good design admin man in Rex Fleming. Also Gordon Sked was a good potential right-hand man in my view. I always felt he had potential, and so I was prepared to put a considerable amount of trust in him. He also had the advantage of being held in high regard by ARG engineering and Product Planning people, and he also knew the company well.

There were casualties, but few people had to be invited to leave. In the event the solution to staffing the new facility was solved, very conveniently, by the decision by Peugeot to close its design and engineering facility at Whitley just down the road in Coventry. This, of course was the old Chrysler facility that I had set up in the early '70s, and I was very well aware of who was there and what their capabilities were.

The majority of the design staff at Whitley did not want to relocate to France, and yet had very limited choices as to how to remain in UK. The fit was perfect, we needed each other and we were able to fill our vacancies at ARG with high calibre people with known capabilities. Of course, Peugeot was not too happy as they had hoped to move these people to France but as they say, it is an ill wind! So, over a period of just over a year the first two priorities were resolved.

One of the most enjoyable experiences I had in my career was to be involved in the formation of automotive design courses at some of the art colleges in England. We had already taken a major role at the post-graduate course at the Royal College of Art in London in the days of Chrysler UK.

At the beginning of my time at Rover, we worked with the Lanchester Polytechnic in Coventry, later to be Coventry University, on its course. The college still produces designers today.

There were two major colleges in the USA, Art Center in California and the Center for Creative Studies in Detroit. I visited these colleges quite frequently while based in Detroit, and they were the colleges where the 'Big Three' American car companies sourced their new design talent.

When my own career in design started out, there were no such colleges, and nowhere teaching design that had any slant towards the automotive sector as it was not considered serious design. It was thought to be cosmetic, a titivation of things engineering, and that was a view held by the engineers in industry too.

Traditionally, in the UK, engineering would frequently present us with a doubtful design with instructions to 'tart this up a bit' which was a very annoying term to use.

Styling was an appropriate title in those days in the sense that it was something that was applied after the design was completed. But the title changed to design when things got a lot more serious and our function began to have an input at the earliest stage of development. It was by one of those incredible sequences of luck and good fortune that I ended up being where I wanted to be, designing cars.

I ended up in that place purely by chance, a one in a million chance, and I often think about all those unfortunate young people who shared my ambition but did not have the breaks. I always responded to any young person or their parents who approached me to ask for my advice about a career in automotive design and I am proud to say that many of those who did, rose to senior positions in the industry.

In the late 1960s, when I was Director of Design at Chrysler UK, I was approached by the Royal College of Art's (RCA) Professor Misha Black. He was in charge of the Industrial Design School because, to his credit, he wanted to set up an automotive design course. I was very, very enthused, and along with Uwe Bahnssen of Ford, we managed to get this thing established and sponsored students through this course.

Later on, I saw the beginnings of the other course set up in Coventry. In both cases, we had to make sure that these colleges were not too engineering oriented.

This was not the object of such courses in our view and that eventually got through to the colleges themselves and things started to work quite smoothly.

When I came back to England in 1982, the Coventry College was already operating very well, and I was pleased by what I found there. It all developed on over the years from taking just a handful of students every year to the situation that exists today where colleges are usually encouraged to take on far more people on these courses than perhaps they should in order to generate the finances but that was better than the alternative, which was to have no students coming in at all!

Since then, other schools have opened up in Germany and other countries, which are turning out very good people. The RCA Masters Degree course has produced some fine graduates, many of whom I had the great pleasure of sponsoring through the Chrysler and Rover set-ups, and they eventually became senior figures in various companies including those I worked in.

In the 1990s, I also became a board member of Birmingham's Polytechnic, which became the University of Central England. I served there, on the board of governors, for many years until the time I retired. It was a great pleasure to do that, to see how these colleges worked internally and what made them tick.

I felt honoured to be awarded a fellowship at the Coventry University and a Doctor of the University award from Birmingham, and these are two things I am very proud of. The fact that these colleges produce such excellent people these days is so satisfying and I am very pleased to have been a part of that, and to see it bear fruit.

We stepped up these training programmes with Coventry and the RCA. With the new design courses, we were able to bring quite a lot of excellent young designers through. All this enabled me to establish a strong design team to staff our new building.

Now, we could concentrate on the product more effectively. All new cars would take at least four years to come through and so short-term measures had to be put into motion to bring together a common visual theme for the existing product line.

There was an excellent product plan developing, starting with the Rover 800, and going on to other new products, which covered the replacement of the range with a new set of products.

These ranged from the Mini/Metro, which would be AR6, through the mid-range AR8, to the upper-medium AR16. There would also be many derivatives on these basic models.

The final Rover 800 in clay.

Rover 800 Fastback model varied little from the final production car.

There was hope that this would also include an MG sports car, but the financial justification of this was difficult at the time, as sports cars had faded from the market and could not be viable. This was according to the finance people, who thought it would fail without a sales outlet in the USA; they were probably right!

I did try to illustrate the MG potential with a derivative of an early small car model, and I think that this and the MG EXE did serve to rekindle the interest internally in MG as a sports car marque. The real tragedy was that such a car was designed and evaluated and could have hit the market 18 months ahead of the Mazda MX-5/Miata.

Both Marketing and Product Planning had to be convinced of the need for a recognizable product image. This did not take too long to achieve and we were soon on the road to creating the first mock-ups to illustrate the plan.

At this time, the relationship with Honda regarding product was unclear.

The first cooperative project was already in place with the Triumph branded Ballade, known as the Acclaim. And doing the same thing using the next generation version resulted in the relatively conservative Rover 213/216. This was a thinly disguised Honda with only the front and rear being changed, but it was a step forward and did allow the application of elements of the new ARG identity and this product proved to be a good seller for ARG as a stop-gap.

The plan for the Rover 800 was to develop a car that was common in mechanical components and structure with the Honda Legend. But the two cars would have a completely different visual image both in exterior and interior design theme.

Axe wanted to right the Maestro's wrongs, and this proposal certainly made the car look a lot more marketable with minimal panel changes.

The Montego was similarly treated to a facelifted rear. It never made production.

The Honda Legend was aimed specifically at the USA market, whereas the Rover version was, initially at least, aimed at the European market.

This task of designing this complex joint product was achieved during 1982 and 1983. It was not easy, as neither company had any previous experience in working this closely with another, and Honda had never built a large car before. The new ARG design studios, and those of Honda, formed a close relationship based on mutual respect and this relationship did not fade over time.

Throughout all this I was given a great deal of autonomy and support from the ARG board. Had all this proceeded to plan, I believe that we would have seen a very different company and one that might well still exist today.

The company was, however, owned by the government, and its priorities were to be more oriented towards the disposal of its 'White Elephant'. As a result, the planned actions did not all take place, and the end result was a mish-mash of new and patched up product that weakened the company's chances of survival.

For Honda, the Legend project was a step into the unknown, and it looked for ARG for guidance. Little did they know! The framework for the project was agreed including the basic dimensions, mechanical layout, known in the business as 'the package'. Levels of commonality were identified, which was that all visible parts of the car were to be individual to each company but that as much of the structure underneath was to be common.

The initial meeting was arranged to take place at Canley between the design and engineering groups of ARG and Honda in order to meet and get to know each other and to discuss the brief. The meeting took place and we, at ARG, felt that it was likely that Honda would show its hand in some way at this meeting as to the direction it was intending to go.

We did not want to be in a position to have to only talk about our views but felt that we needed to have something to show if only as an 'aunt sally' basis for this important discussion. I felt this should be a full-size model in Fibreglass but time to do this was very tight.

We had agreed that the meeting would be in the old Canley studio, as it was close to the HQ offices and was really the only place that we could exhibit something like a full-size model.

This early model was completed in record time, and was ready for the meeting. Honda's design director and a small team of his people, plus the Honda Chairman and senior engineers with interpreters, came over and after preliminaries the model was uncovered. To our great surprise, Honda's work to date was of a mechanical nature and they had nothing to show regarding the body, so in fact, both parties were surprised.

The Honda people were impressed and the model proved to be very helpful in providing a focus for the meeting, and proved to be absolutely the right thing to do.

The meeting went very well and the design (styling) teams got on particularly well. The basics of the programme as it related to the design and engineering operations of both companies were approved in principle and we were ready to go.

After that meeting, each company worked up their own proposals, and a follow up meeting took place at Canley between the relevant parties. The

AR6 taster model was shown, unannounced, at the opening of the Canley studios.

design group meetings, again, went very well, and I had arranged an evening at my house for the two teams to get to know each other socially.

This working relationship worked well though all of the joint-programme work done in the next few years. My opposite number at Honda, Shinya Iwakura, became a close colleague and a good friend over the years to come. Iwakura declared, at the second XX meeting, to the great amusement of particularly the engineers present, that he and I were now 'married'.

The final work on the Rover and Honda clay models, in order to achieve the commonality of the touchdown points, where the exterior met the interior, was done at Canley. It was decided to do it there because of the way the engineering responsibilities between Honda and BL were assigned.

We had a real problem working out how to do this initially as, of course, we had no suitable facility to do the work in, the new facility not yet being complete. The old buildings were woefully inadequate and no one even considered utilising the elephant house over in Longbridge, because it was such a rundown building and quite unsuitable for purpose. All we had was the partially completed facility at Canley and this was behind the existing smaller studio.

The first set of surface plates were being put into the ground, these plates or rails are the base from which the clay model's detailed measurements would be taken and we were able to partition off the rest of the new building and open the doors between the old building and the new section.

These plates were used to do the work on the two projects, the Honda and Rover clay models being worked side by side and these two models were finalised and certified together in that location.

It made life very difficult for us as we still had other projects to work on, there were still all the other cars Rover made all of which needed to be updated and this work had to be screened from the Japanese designers. I can't remember working in more difficult conditions, but when we visited the Honda design studios in Tokyo later on, rather surprisingly they did not have grandiose design facilities either and, therefore, the work was done in good spirit by both groups, with both proposals approved by their respective boards on time.

I had a number of interesting comments from the Japanese designers and engineers who confided in me. They said that they preferred our design to theirs. What a wonderful opportunity it would have been to build our cars to Japanese levels of engineering and manufacturing quality. It would have produced a very fine product and could well have saved the company from its eventual fate. That was one of those great missed opportunities.

Aborted Montego replacement, known as AR17 had fewer compromises than the car it had been designed to follow onto the marketplace.

AR17 five-door would have been pitched at the upper end of the Sierra sector.

Market research was a dominant factor with our model, but I believe much less so with the Honda if at all. We must remember that the first Legend was aimed squarely at the USA, as its domestic market was quite small for cars in this sector.

The market research done by our company was detailed and painfully meticulous, the car was gone over in fine detail by teams of people who were brought in and studied our cars alongside the de-badged opposition in clinics.

Cars were evaluated in terms of front, rear and side views, and every detail you could think of, and these results were worked out, correlated.

A gentleman who specialised in this type of work would then stand up in front of the Board and interpret the results.

The results were very favourable for our car, but that can be a rather disquieting thing because sometimes it is better to have the public feel there is some controversy in the design that it's too advanced to be comfortable with it right away.

If they are too comfortable with it,

then it means that they are comfortable *now*, and none of those people are really qualified to project their thinking ahead four years, and be able to see what the future holds. After all, that's what a designer does.

Designers were so often hamstrung in this area by this type of market research but, thankfully, research today is done in a very different way.

The relationship between ARG and Honda engineering was much less harmonious and there were many disagreements on both the mechanical specs and the body construction details. Honda threw in the occasionally 'wobbly' too.

One example of this was that at quite a late stage they suddenly informed us that the angle of the back upper edge of the door line above the waist did not comply with the limousine rules for entry in Japan. This was serious for them, as the Legend in Japan had to comply.

I can only assume that Honda had overlooked this, and it made for quite a big problem to resolve, as the doors and inner structure were all involved on both cars. The problem was resolved, and these things happen but relationships can be strained.

Many trips to Japan were required. The interiors of the two designs were totally different in design; the ARG design was deliberately based on themes from the earlier Rover cars, and one of the earliest design alternatives had strong approval from everyone. In order to accommodate the common structure required in the firewall area it was found that our design for the dashboard area would have to be raised some inches to make the commonality possible.

Despite our worst fears, this worked out to the advantage of the design in the end, but it caused some sleepless nights at the time!

With the initial styling work complete, we turned our attention to the completion of the new studios. The company wanted to use this new

Roy Axe wanted sporting cars to be unique to the MG marque as this early R8 coupé proposal shows.

XX packaging did throw up one or two problems that were lost in translation.

The Canley studio had its own showroom.

facility immediately to illustrate to the press that things had changed radically from the old days. The company now had a state of the art design premises and we wanted to show it off.

It was down to the tremendous efforts of Bob Neville that got the project through, and that we managed to achieve this so quickly. Harold had tried to get me to temper my plans, modify things we already had rather than have new equipment, but when I reminded him of what he promised in our interview before I joined the company, he agreed that he had promised and that was what would be done. Bob Neville was instrumental in making sure that this all went through on a very modest budget, but nevertheless we managed to do it.

We had a very workable and spacious facility as a result but not a very attractive showpiece from the outside, which still looked like the old factory building that it was as it was built within the upper end of the factory behind the old Canley office buildings.

These old office buildings were refurbished (a relative term) and used for the company HQ, and inside the offices were better than they'd ever been before but not exactly a showpiece. Our new design facility was big enough to accommodate all our design personnel with room for future expansion and with a foyer that made up somewhat for the surroundings of the old building. The press would be routed in through this foyer without access to the offices.

We were concerned about the launch of the facility; after all, what did we have to show to the press other than the interior of the building? They could look at the space and see what the layout was and the equipment but we had very little to show them other than Rover 800s covered over with sheets, and the only vehicles that were able to be exposed were the old tired ones that the press had not been too kind to.

There was also the odd Maestro around, which wasn't too inspirational to anybody

The R8 range would go on sale in late 1989 to much critical acclaim.

either. We used the more dramatic versions of the SD1, the Vitesse, but nevertheless there was still something missing, excitement and titillation! We had a project that we had completed in design, which was intended as a stimulus to the designers we had, who were weary of working on Montego and Maestro.

They had needed some encouragement too and we had designed and produced a fibre-glass model of a Metro sized car. I obtained the agreement from Harold with the enthusiastic support of PR to leave the model uncovered in the studio as something that would intrigue the press. We would not identify or talk about it, it would just be there and the press would not be allowed to photograph it. In the event, this worked quite well, it stirred up the interest of the press and we had a good launch with the press gathered in the showroom for a verbal presentation by myself followed by a question and answer session.

We talked through what we were doing and what was going on, and it all went down very well. Many of the press present at this meeting were people I knew from my previous life with Chrysler in Europe, and I knew them very well in some cases.

This was a comfortable meeting as far as I was concerned but it was difficult to get across what we were doing with so little new to show in terms of product, after all when you're a designer, those properties are your means of communication.

15

The ARG Showcar Projects: 1984–1985

THE MG EX-E

IHAVE NOT MADE ANY special reference to show cars in the Chrysler Europe and USA days as these things are usually done for PR or marketing reasons. The special projects we did at ARG were rather different however as they were done, at least the first one, against the initial wishes of the usual supporters.

There had been delays in the ARG XX project, which had not affected Honda with the Legend, meaning the Japanese car would now be announced first. Harold Musgrove, quite rightly, would not release the 800 until he was satisfied that it would meet the high standards the company had set for quality.

In the event, it never did, and Harold had to yield to pressures from the government to put the 800 on sale prematurely, which was, to say the least, unfortunate. I promoted the idea of producing a show car.

With the delays for the 800 becoming apparent, and knowing it was going to slip back further, we knew that the difficulty of press credibility was going to grow. So I talked to Harold about the prospect of creating a show car that we could display on an auto show stand as an example of the kind of work we were capable of.

I felt that I should really pressure to create and show an exciting exhibit for the international show circuit. There was nothing happening otherwise than the less than exciting introduction of the Maestro and Montego. I felt that the company needed a shot in the arm, something that would excite the press and create global interest; something unexpected.

I also needed something to say to the design fraternity that ARG had new facilities that could compete worldwide in order to attract the calibre of new people I needed for the work yet to come. I owned a Ferrari 308 at the time, and felt that a sports car of this type but updated would show that England was just as capable as anyone of producing a car with worldwide appeal.

Sales & Marketing were against the idea, as ARG did not make such cars, and the fear that it could prove to be a sales distraction. Harold Musgrove was enthusiastic, though, but also was aware of the marketing position and could not ignore it, he felt the project had too many downsides to go ahead fully.

After more discussions, however, it was agreed that we should proceed with the design, aiming to reveal it at the Frankfurt Motor Show of 1984. The model was to be made more credible by creating a chassis and mechanical specification to complement the styling, and the engine chosen was the one being developed for the MG Metro 6R4 rally car.

Spen King from the Gaydon experimental department was brought in to work out the chassis details, and we in design worked with Spen to develop a proposal. Up to that

Richard Hamblin, Roy Axe and Gordon Sked with the EX-E

point I did not really know Spen, but had been an admirer from afar so to speak. Spen was and is a man with very strong opinions and I think it is fair to say that so do I!

As a result, a number of vigorous discussions took place, as we battled for a package that would retain the drama of a world-class concept car. I enjoyed working with Spen, and it was a real regret on my part that the opportunity to do much more with him did not arise again, other than the use of the small car body design mentioned earlier, on the ECV3.

The visual goal was for a sporting GT of generally Ferrari 308 size and proportions, but with a totally unique look. We decided that the MG name was the only appropriate one to use.

I am an aircraft enthusiast and a follower of military style, if that is the right term. I was very impressed by the F16 Falcon fighter of the time with its command pilot position and surrounding bubble canopy, and this was the inspiration I gave to the design team.

The design manager for the exterior of the project was Gordon Sked and the small team of designers included the new college grads Richard Woolley and David Saddington; and also Gerry McGovern who was new to the company, having joined from Peugeot. I had hired Gerry directly from school, as covered earlier, as something of an experiment, years earlier at Chrysler UK.

The project started well, but then got bogged down as such projects often do. I remember one weekend morning, getting the team together and thrashing out some of the forms. The shape had become heavy, and I felt it should take a cue from the 308, and have the bonnet surface below the wings creating a lighter look and the great view forward from the cockpit that I so admired in the Ferrari.

We removed a lot of clay from the model that day, and the problems were sorted out. The form that eventually became the final model emerged in the three dimensional development.

The interior team was led by Richard Hamblin, who had recently joined us from Ogle as chief of interior design. Here, we were after a totally unique and high-tech look to reflect the new technology that was emerging but at the same time keeping a theme of sports car driver involvement. Head-up displays and computer readouts were incorporated.

MG EX-E had supercar proportions.

The final sketches used in the publicity covering the design process were, in fact, produced after the event, as it were. Gerry McGovern was involved in the project and did those final sketches, but in fairness to the others he was not the only designer involved, it was very much a team effort.

Specialised Mouldings of Huntingdon, who was producing our fibreglass models at that time, cast the silver-painted model, and it looked fantastic. There was still the resistance to showing it, until I unveiled the final finished model to Harold Musgrove. He was convinced and Marketing were won over too and with just a few days to the show opening at Frankfurt in 1984, he instructed that the model would be shown.

The results are there to see by referring to the press reports of the time, the car received a wonderful reception, and ARG was the subject of much speculation for the future. The show model is still around and when I last saw it at the Gaydon museum I felt a great deal of personal satisfaction for the design which has, I feel, stood the test of time well and would not look out of place if introduced today, though this is, I admit, a very biased opinion! Needless to say a few people who had sat on the sidelines or took a very minor role in promoting the project were quick to associate themselves with the EX-E but that is the way of the world!

THE ROVER CCV

The ice was broken and there was little opposition to the idea of doing another show car for the following year. This time, there was more focus on the design theme to support the Rover 800 which was well along the path to production and plans were forming to re-enter the USA market.

For the USA a two-door coupé would have been much preferable to the four-door, but plans and funds available did not support this as its appeal would have mainly been in the USA, and volumes would be restricted. There were better places to use the limited use of funds available, or so it was judged. The idea of a two-door coupé show car, however, had good support and so we started out on this project due for release at the 1985 Turin show.

Essentially the same design teams were used, but with a few changes, due to the original EX-E people being involved in other things. The design office again set the parameters, and I felt that the coupé should pick up the character of the 800 saloon in terms of basic form and character lines, but without the restrictions on dimensions due to its commonality with the Honda Legend.

The extra form at front and rear allied with the more shapely sides greatly enhanced the 800-based lines. The joint XX programme with Honda had a maximum width limitation due to Japanese regulations. Of course, with a show car, designers are also spared the restrictions of current production technology and cost considerations.

I also felt the car should reflect some of the character of the MG EX-E in terms of the transparent roof. In this case the roof was not as radical as the EX-E due to the proportions and end use considerations of a coupé, but the idea worked and the design came together effortlessly around these guide lines and the final result, both interior and exterior, were very much to everyone's satisfaction.

As with the EX-E, the final result just looked right, and it sailed through the approval process with no changes. It was exactly as we had intended it to be and that cleared it for exhibition at the show in Turin.

This model was built by MGA in Coventry, a company who we were to work with closely from then on. Again, the reaction can be read in the publications of the day, and were all most complimentary. To get such a good reception in Italy was a particular pleasure and I received many compliments for the car from the Italian designers.

Regrettably, this was the last of the show cars, as the years immediately following had the design office fully occupied with the new product plan.

This is not to say that designs were not explored that could have been the subject of show vehicles and a number of models were built. But there just was not the same need to do this in the climate of new production model introductions.

At least four MG sports car projects were explored as design office ideas, which were taken to full-size fibreglass models to try to stimulate the resurrection of the MG marque. All fell by the wayside due to lack of support for these programmes, as they were not considered financially viable, though the designs were greatly admired within the company.

Not until the MGF was conceived, incorporating many of the ideas and details of these earlier designs, was the MG marque to be given the vehicle it deserved. It is sad to think that one very good design for a small MG could have easily seen the light of day almost two years before the Mazda Miata (MX-5) made everyone worldwide realise that such a product could be viable and would contribute a great deal to any company's image in the world markets.

It is fair to say, however, that without the US market, the Mazda Miata would not have enjoyed quite so much success and even then we do not really know if this was a profitable programme for Mazda or

F16 Concept was not pursued, but would lead to greater things during the '90s.

AR6-based Midget also failed to progress beyond full-scale model stage.

one they have used to assist in the perception of the rest of their range of products. Either way it was an excellent project for them and another lost opportunity for us.

Such is life, and it also illustrates the frustrations in the design business when designers often have the 'feel' for what is right, but cannot get the idea past the company analysts.

The PR department at Rover was always very supportive of the new design office. In the early days, it was something of a godsend, I would think, as we did have things going on that they could talk to the press about.

They made the most of the MG EX-E and the Rover CCV and would very much have liked to continue with a show car programme, but this was the end of these projects, all hands being put to work on production projects. I might add as a footnote that the government owners of ARG were also against the 'waste of money' for such projects which is another illustration of politicians and industry being a bad mix!

16

BMIHT and Personal Cars: 1982–1992

HAROLD ASKED ME IF I would join the board of trustees of the BMIHT (British Motor Industry Heritage Trust) operation, which was based in an old Manor House out at Studley Castle. The main building was being used as a Marketing and Sales school, but the outbuildings were filled with a collection of old cars, comprised of the marques from Austin Rover's constituent companies.

It was an impressive collection but some of it was quite dilapidated, as there was not a lot of money for its upkeep. BMIHT also had a core of really old vehicles in excellent condition, a number of which were pre-1910, with a few that were pre-1904. Therefore, they had Brighton run eligibility and the Heritage Trust put these vehicles in the world famous run on a regular basis.

The Heritage's MD was Peter Mitchell. He was a great enthusiast and an excellent man for the job. Peter had an excellent assistant in David Bishop. The board was made up of people who had got involved over the years; Alex Park from the old days of BL was on the Board and also a great enthusiast; Brigadier Charles Maple, who was in charge of the audit system in the main company; and Ron Lucas, who was retired and who formerly had been with the company in the USA. These people had to be applauded because they had saved these cars from being lost forever.

There was also a small cadre of very dedicated staff to administer and look after the vehicles. However all the members of the board were not really interested in the cars, and Peter was always pleased to have someone there like me, who was a true car enthusiast and knew something about the cars, their values and place in history.

Roy Axe on the London to Brighton run

Peter and I had many enjoyable discussions and I could back him up on many of the things he wanted to do with the vehicles. The board was reconstituted, with ARG Chairman Harold Musgrove in overall charge.

I was on the Board of Trustees for a number of years, right through to the time Les Wharton joined as the new MD of what by then had been renamed The Rover Group. Les put a great deal of personal effort into establishing a new museum to put all these vehicles in, because they were in the most appalling storage conditions over at Studley.

He raised about £8m, if I remember rightly, in order to build an all-new museum, which was built at Gaydon. It was also the place where we decided to store all of our old fibreglass models from the design studios, as well as many others from well before my time and this became a fascinating group of first prototypes and 'could have beens', many of which still exist.

This was really a very significant achievement by Les, and the fact that it happened in such difficult times is very much to his credit. Tony Rose was the finance director at the time, and he gave a great deal of support to the project and as I have said previously, it always pays to have the finance man with you!

One of the perks of being on the board was that I was able to drive some of the old vehicles in the London to Brighton Run, and I took part in quite a few of these events. They were enormous fun to do. It was a great pleasure to drive these old cars, and indeed to learn to drive them, and then to take them out on to the road.

The Brighton Run is held in November and often ends up being rainy, and can be exhausting physic- ally, depending on which car you're driving. Soon after I joined the board of trustees, Peter Mitchell asked me if I would drive the 1899 Wolseley that the trust owned. This car competed in the 1000-mile trials, I think in 1904, and it was quite a primitive thing, steered by tiller.

It was quite small with only seats for two with most of the controls grouped around the right hand side. This included the 'clutch', which was a long lever with a button on the end, which slackened off the belt and allowed the gears to be changed, the throttle was also on that side and in fact you needed five right arms and one left arm to drive the thing at all. Quite an experience when driving it in modern traffic!

There were effectively no brakes and the driver had to be careful not to go too fast downhill, or the vehicle became uncontrollable. A steady nerve was required and you had to drive the car in a very particular way, it was an altogether more methodical process than driving a modern car.

Peter asked me if I would go out to Studley one Sunday morning and try the car out. This was quite an experience, I managed to get the vehicle going okay, but I really doubted whether I could handle it all the way down to Brighton, even with the back-up crew following along.

On the night before the event, my wife Pat and I duly set off to London and had dinner with the other competitors, many of whom had done numerous trips before. We were pretty raw and really didn't know what to expect, however, we were pitched in at the deep end, and we set off on a misty morning out of Hyde Park at an unearthly hour and crossed the Thames and through southern London.

Halfway to Brighton, we stopped for a very good breakfast laid on by the Trust. We did well on the first half of the trip, and had few problems and arrived in quite good time without too many mishaps.

The car was extremely underpowered, and did not enjoy going up any kind of hill, however we managed to get up all of them without my wife having to get out and push! We didn't feel under any urgent pressure to continue after breakfast as we were in good shape for time (we learned from this trip for later events!)

When we did set off on the second half of the trip, events developed into a series of incidents. Our first one happened when we came to an angled crossroads and as we approached, a policeman stepped out and held up the traffic and waved us across. We drove across, not slackening speed but about halfway across there was an enormous 'BOING' noise and a 'JING, JING, JING', and a 'CLUNK, CLUNK, CLUNK' before the car finally went 'DUNGA, DUNGA, DUNGA' and came to a halt.

We had no idea what had happened and were sitting there wondering what to do next, when the policeman appeared on Pat's side of the car holding a very large piece of cast iron in his hand, which I guess was the flywheel. He said to my wife, 'I think Madam that this component might cause you a little trouble on the rest of your run!' What an understatement!

We thought this was the end of our trip. However, the back-up team arrived and they re-assembled the car at the side of the road, and before too long we were able to continue. After a couple more similar but less severe incidents, we continued on and eventually managed to get into Brighton, and made it just inside the timeframe. This was a very long day's drive and a very tiring but exhilarating trip.

I drove this car on the Brighton run several times, once with my son Chris. The car was not going well that day, and Chris had to leap out and push when we were going uphill and the car was obviously down on power. In the end, it completely died, and there was nothing that could be done, the engine had to be rebuilt. The car's registration was OWL 707 and 'little owl' was remembered by spectators from year to year, and cheered along every inch of the way.

I also got to drive the Trust's 1904 Wolseley on a couple of occasions. Four people were able to sit in (I should say on) this much bigger car; it was yellow, with the luxury of a steering wheel. Gear changing was not particularly easy, but nothing like as difficult as the older car. We had two or three good runs down in that. It was all a very good experience.

There were other cars in the collection, the Rover Meteor was one, and I remember doing one rally in it with Pat. I also did a few runs in MG Old Number One, which wasn't really the original at all, but more of a replica. But it was an old replica and looked perfectly genuine.

I drove this car with considerable difficulty, taking it on the Shakespeare Run around Warwickshire. I had to drive it alone because the cockpit was so narrow and the seats were staggered so that I couldn't get anyone else in the car with me (If I had been thinner it might have helped).

Also the distance between the front of the seat cushion and the pedals was so short that I could not drive the car for any great distance without getting severe cramp, and I ended up perfecting a system by which I drove the car crossed-legged for much of the time.

This way I gained a little extra legroom in order to operate the clutch and the accelerator. You sure have to think about what you are doing when you drive a car cross-legged!

It was a very enjoyable experience with the BMIHT's cars, and I had a good time too, helping Peter seek out other cars to buy, and which cars in the collection we should dispose of.

Peter and I were considered the two who were most qualified to decide what should be kept and what should go when rationalising the collection, and the other Trustees formally gave us that responsibility.

Around the time I came back to England, I thought it was time to enjoy a car of my own. Since the late 1960s I have had countless company cars, and quite a few competitive cars to drive some of which were very high quality.

I was familiar with Mercedes-Benz, BMW, and with many luxury and high performance cars, particularly when I was in the USA, so I had a pretty broad experience of a wide range of cars.

These cars however were not mine, and I decided when I came back to England I'd buy myself a Ferrari 308. I've always been

The second of Roy Axe's Ferrari Boxers.

very keen on Ferrari and very keen on Pininfarina, whom I rate as one of the finest Italian coachbuilders, with a fine track record particularly in the period when Leonardo Fioravanti was Design Director.

I am sure that the current Chairman of Pininfarina would not be offended if I said he did not design the cars personally. He has a design director and design team, and those people are not always well publicised certainly the most famous in recent years has been Leonardo Fioravanti, who has designed every good modern Ferrari, from the Daytona to the Boxer. The 308 and all the other good show cars of that era were also his. Leonardo's a charming man, who I have met on a number of occasions, and who is still around designing cars independently.

The Ferrari 308 was a car I admired a great deal, so I duly bought one. This led to a period of time when I owned a number of Ferraris, changing them every couple of years or so through to Boxers and eventually a Testarossa. I generally mixed and matched as I went along.

Also at that time, I bought another car I had admired for a long time, an Austin-Healey 3000. Nigel Dawes, who operated near Malvern in Worcestershire, rebuilt this car for me and I really enjoyed it. In fact I owned it longer than any other car, and only just recently sold it because of lack of use. It was kept in England and I am not there very often so I just did not get to use it enough. My Ferrari and Healey ownership were times I really enjoyed.

Gerry Coker designed the Healey 100 and Sprite, and when I was in Florida some years ago, I enquired with a car restorer friend, Gene Cohen, if he knew anything about this man.

Gerry left Healey soon after the Sprite was launched, and went to work for Chrysler in the USA. This was before I worked for Chrysler. Gerry worked for them as a styling engineer, and had never become a stylist with Chrysler, which I thought was an incredible waste of talent.

After all, when he was with Healey, he not only styled the body, but he engineered it, too. He'd left by the time I got there and had gone to Ford. I heard on the grapevine that he had retired in Florida, and that meant he must have been close by. My friend Gene said, 'I know Gerry well, in fact, he is down in our part of Florida and he lives really close to where you do.' A quarter of a mile away, no less, but he had just sold up and moved to North Carolina.

I didn't meet him then, but I did catch up with him later, because he moved back, spending his winters in Florida and his summers in North Carolina. Gene set up a dinner with our respective wives and Pat and I struck a good friendship with Gerry and his wife Marion right away.

Because Gerry had gone through an apprenticeship at Rootes in a very similar way to me, though some years before, we had a lot in common. We have become good friends and he still lives close to us in Sarasota in the winter months and I see him fairly frequently. We share car magazines and other things together, and it was one of those enormous pleasures to get to know him as the man who was the inspiration behind my Healey. This gave our friendship a special meaning too.

There are a lot of car designers around here, and many more visit Florida in the winter. It's good to have lunch with them from time to time. There is also a thriving British car community, The Suncoast British Car Club, which has about 100 members, and a lot of interesting cars. It features a diverse range spanning Triumph 1800s, an Alvis sports car of the '50s, and many other fascinating vehicles. There are plenty of car shows to see here too, and the popularity of old British cars in the USA is very impressive.

I also want to make a special tribute to a man I never met but much admired. This is another Gerald, Gerald Palmer. He was a designer of cars' mechanical and bodywork and his two great contributions in my view were the 1950's Jowett Javlin and the later MG Magnette. A small volume of his work titled *Auto-Architect* is well worth a read, a remarkable man.

One of the pleasures of being the Design Director was that I had the first drive in almost all competitive cars brought into the company to evaluate. Very often it was a case of driving a different car every night. This was in addition to the fact that I had a company car issued free, and which was changed regularly.

These company cars were usually the top-of-the-range, and when I joined Rover,

Jaguar was still in the group, and that meant that Directors had an XJ Series III saloon. This was a beautiful car to drive, it was something my wife, daughter and I all enjoyed it was just so smooth and comfortable.

We did a lot of miles in the different ones we had, I think we had five or six of them over a period of time, and it was a very good experience. There was a negative side to it as well, of course, and that was that Jaguars were invariably let down by poor quality. The press garages used to have to spend a lot of time sorting out Directors' cars, as it was deemed not to be a good thing for a company director to have his car break down in some public place!

Later on we moved to Rover SD1s after Jaguar had been privatised, and these cars were considered to be quite a climb down. Needless to say though, a well-sorted SD1 Vitesse was a very fine car to have once a decent round steering wheel was fitted and the car was virtually rebuilt by the press garage! This was not really such a good thing because the Directors were effectively insulated from the real experience of owning one of these cars and experiencing the quality shortcomings that regular customers experienced.

I remember that one of my Vitesses was built in a special colour combination, black with special trim (again, such things are a perk of being the Design Director). The car was very well finished off, with its stripes and other things such as special wheels. This car was just about finished, and about to be delivered to me and I was really looking forward to receiving it. Then I received that fateful call from the press garage: They had put the car through the car wash and one of the rollers came off and ran amok, demolishing the whole front end of 'my' car.

There we were with a £15,000 car with all the special work done on it effectively smashed to pieces, a very unfortunate occurrence. It was rebuilt, of course and I did take delivery of it, but it didn't seem amusing at the time, even if it does now.

17

The Decline and Fall of ARG: 1985–1986

LOOKING BACK AT IT now, it's difficult to believe that only four and a half years after I joined the company Harold Musgrove resigned. It seemed like such a very long time, and I guess that's because we were working together closely through a busy and productive time. In the early days, the atmosphere was decidedly optimistic, and I suppose this was because of the way Michael Edwardes had finally defeated the unions.

At last, it seemed, we would be able to get rid of that load of baggage from the past, and to get into the business of managing a car company again. Sadly Edwardes only went so far, I guess the time available did not allow him to completely rationalise the assembly plants to reduce the vast overheads.

Going back to the 1950s, the companies that eventually formed BMC and later BL were at one point, producing something like 70 per cent of the cars in the UK. As things evolved, Austin and Morris, the two biggest companies merged and formed BMC, which was a truly huge company, but which was not integrated in terms of its management or the philosophy of its people or products.

This was a difficult situation, which was never really resolved. In fact, when I joined the company in 1982 after further mergers, this division between what was Austin and Morris, although somewhat blurred by then, was very definitely still there. It created an atmosphere that was not total togetherness, and the company never really had the focus it needed. By this time, Triumph and Rover were also merged in as a sort of up market division but this all changed.

I think this is visible in the product when looking at the cars produced in, say, the 1970s; they all seemed to owe something to one part or another of one of the companies that went on to form BL as a whole. This resulted in a very disparate range of cars. A company like Ford had applied a corporate theme to the style of its range, and the same was the case with Vauxhall. But in the case of BMC, and later BL, it was a fragmented picture, making it difficult to connect the brands to one company. While this had some good points to it, one of them being individuality, overall it was a very negative situation. It failed to make BL appear on the roads as the large manufacturer that it was.

These problems were still there in 1982. The failure to rationalise the plants, and the failure to address manufacturing quality and general undesirability of the product all contributed to this music hall joke that was BL.

When I returned to the UK, people would burst out laughing when I said I worked for BL, it was a total joke. It was also quite tragic if you think of the sheer number of plants that were in existence, and the people they employed. The company had addressed the situation at Canley (ex-Triumph) and Solihull, where Land Rover was the only vehicle produced at that plant, but overall, it was ludicrous to have this number of factories across the country. Especially considering the greatly reduced market share the company held.

Ironically the Japanese started to appear on the scene in British manufacturing. First Nissan then Honda and Toyota, all backed by local government to entice them into non-traditional areas for the industry. It was interesting that the Japanese made this work unlike the British-owned companies during the 1950s! These factories were modern, efficient and nowhere near as labour intensive as BL. There was no need to ship cars or parts around the country, in a way that was guaranteed to produce damage and inefficiencies.

BL was producing some quite old engines that did not have a very good warranty reputation, and if you have products that call heavily on their warranties, then you're going to have a massive drain on the company's finances. Not to mention the customers who get heartily fed up going back to the dealership and complaining about their cars. There were also far too many dealers who were far from polite in trying to solve these problems.

This is all very well, so long as everybody is producing products of a similar standard, but once you're up against people who have got over that situation, then you are in immediate trouble if you don't get your act together. The solution, heavily influenced by government ownership of the company, was to simply take the plants that already existed, try and strip out the interiors and re-equip with new tooling to manufacture cars with the minimum use of people.

This was fine, in its way, but you needed to be sure that the product was engineered correctly and that the robots were made and programmed correctly.

You also needed to be sure that the plants were streamlined enough to produce these cars in the way the competitors were. It was not possible to close plants as there were obvious political difficulties in doing this and ARG was in a difficult position resulting from all of this.

It's a fact that there is a mindset that develops with many leaders of large industries. It's a very difficult thing for such a leader to say that they are not up to scratch, and they

AR6, or the Metro that never was due for a 1990 launch, but was cancelled.

are not producing as good quality of product they should. That is an admission of failure, which many CEOs of companies in the UK and USA seem to find difficult to make. If we look at GM's current mess, it's a similar scenario: multiple plants scattered across the country trying to compete with purpose-built Japanese and European plants, it's all very familiar to me.

There was almost a Gung-ho attitude in the manufacturing division at BL that said, 'we have been the world's manufacturers for donkey's years, and we invented a lot of

Another AR6 proposal, and one that failed to gain management approval.

This AR6 proposal wearing Rover badges looked complicated to produce.

these things, and no one does it better than we do'.

It was a blinkers-on approach to the whole problem, despite the design (or the attempted design) of much more straightforward cars for manufacture, such as the Rover 800. It was still not possible to make cars of a quality and reliability standard that matched the competition, which included Honda.

This was a great disappointment, and eventually it resulted in Harold Musgrove having to leave the company. The previous failures were not Harold's fault. In fact, I find it impossible to fault him in terms of his dedication to the company. He was committed to the nth degree and full credit must be given to him for this. He tried so hard that it wound him up on occasions, and he could get very emotional and upset with people, and you could understand why.

Luckily Harold had a sense of humour, so if you were someone he had a bit of time for, it was possible to interrupt him in full flow with some diffusing remark, which would calm down the situation and I frequently found myself in that role!

Things could get very tense, and were unpleasant in terms of the endless meetings going on to try and build the products to acceptable quality levels. Now bear in mind that the two newest products were the Maestro and Montego, and you'll understand the problem. They were both disastrously designed for production, and were designed in a way that meant they could never match Japanese quality standards. They were also not up to the competition with regard to appearance. That was problem number one, but there was also the issue of the older products coming down the line, such as the Metro and the Rover SD1.

They were products designed in the old way of doing things, even though the new way of doing things at Rover wasn't a heck of a lot better! This was a time of great frustration but it was also a time of excitement, with the new models coming through the design process.

Ironically, Harold was let down by the engineering and production side, the very groups that he had told me at my original interview with him were under control and who just needed a good design to get their teeth into! The good news was that the company did make a modest profit in the short term, and all of a sudden it was possible to start thinking in terms of the future.

When I joined the company, the situation was such that survival was a major concern, and it was only because of government support that it didn't go under. We tackled the long-range plan with the product planning people with a view to trying to achieve a new image that was consistent.

In the days before I joined, new models were produced one at a time, and I did not get the idea that there was any feeling that the models were looked at as a family to influence the company's future. In fact, just before I joined, there was a premium division in existence, which consisted of Jaguar Rover and Triumph, and then there were the higher volume cars below.

The two ranges were not related as far as overall image was concerned. Once they were pulled together, with the exception of Jaguar and Land Rover, who were about to be spun off, there was a range of vehicles I felt we could tackle, giving them a visual identification linking them to the parent company.

What was needed was a sense that the range as a whole had a corporate identity. And that's why the design processes I introduced were successful, because we could develop ideas, and show them clearly to management. Was also had capacity, finally, to develop cars in parallel.

Never before had fibreglass styling models of prototypes been produced in a way that would enable a range of cars that were some way out in the future, to be looked at all together in full size. But now, the full impact of what the customer of the future would be able to see was available for the company management to appreciate.

AR18 coupé proposal built convincingly in glass fibre.

One of the first things I did was to ensure that all of our new car models were produced in this way, and in some cases just a broad idea of what an upcoming model would look like was enough to put the whole range into context.

We could produce a Metro-sized car, right up to a big Rover, and show how they could all be linked visually together. This did not mean a series of vehicles all looking exactly the same in different sizes, but it meant that the DNA was clearly visible across the range.

Of course we were stuck at the very beginning with the Maestro and Montego. We really had a problem updating those cars as soon as we reasonably could in order to give them some semblance of belonging before the new models came on stream. This was where all of the activity lay particularly between product planning and design. Marketing did play a part, but in the initial stages we were given quite a free hand to put these ideas together and present them to the management committee.

Metro facelift proved a disappointment for Roy Axe.

This was how the pressure was applied to get a cohesive range of cars, not too complex but vehicles that could be recognized in the sense that the Ford model range could be identified as being products of the same company. There was a lot of debate about which model sectors needed to be included in the range, however, and the waters were being muddied by the new relationship with Honda.

The original plan was that certain cars from each company should share components that were hidden from view but the parts that were in view should retain the identities of the companies selling the products. Three years on, ARG, whose fortunes were being dragged down by the Maestro/Montego problems, could no longer afford the manpower to follow the philosophy that was originally envisaged for its relationship with Honda.

The unreliability bug was really beginning to bite and soak up engineering resources. The engineering department claimed it wasn't large enough to be able to put out the fires on the cars in production and at the same time be in a position to put any manpower into the design of new bodies.

It was relatively simple to lean on Honda for the mechanical components, but the bodies were supposed to be unique, and there was not the capacity to handle that. Michael Edwards' initial plans for the BL-Honda deal were to bring the new joint products to market as quickly as possible.

We finally got to the situation with the Rover 800 and Legend, the XX and HX programme, where the cars were visually separated in the way that companies wanted to go. However, soon after that, there was neither the money nor the resources to continue with that philosophy, and it fell back to the situation where Honda and Rover shared a large number of the body panels, and other key surface areas.

Rover 800 facelift didn't go far enough in developing the original's early lead in the marketplace. It soon fell behind its rivals after a strong start.

This made life more difficult in terms of applying individual imagery to the Rover vehicle. The Rover 800 had been in production for only a short time (due to a late launch) when we were confronted by the fact that Honda was about to introduce a second generation Legend. They had changed a great many parts in the car so there were no longer as many commonalities between the two cars.

Austin Rover could not afford to replace the 800 at this point, and the original plan was to replace it after a maximum of six years ... which was now. Honda could no longer wait for Rover to decide whether it was able to repeat what was done with the 800, and Legend went its own way and 800 had to continue with its original design.

In fact, during the life of the 800, there were three different Legends and only one major facelift for the Rover. The Rover model remained in production for some 13 years, which illustrates clearly why Rover sales declined. The car was a really old design at the end, and the original intention to produce a car that would be in production for six years before being replaced, was abandoned. Just like in the old BL days. This was the start of the bad times again.

One of the reasons I and many others in the company believed the quality would be right on the 800, was the huge amount of money being invested in robotic assembly in the Cowley. This was going ahead at a fast pace. There was also the application of CAD within design, engineering and manufacturing, another very large investment.

The effect of CAD in the early stages of a new model's development was dramatic, and can best be described here by an explanation of how the work was done up to that point in time and how it would be done with the assistance of CAD. I should explain that design in this sense meant the engineering definitions of the sheet metal components that design (styling) had produced plus the inner metal structure.

I have already explained earlier the changes in procedure and the development of a database that could be controlled. This had helped a great deal but the structural design and components of the body were still required to fit and this was not yet fully integrated into the procedure. The transition to this system was what was taking place at ARG when I joined, and a very large amount of money was being spent on this.

I also felt that the methods being used to approve designs, which were being produced in the traditional way with the design committee signing off on the clay model and with the design committee also having the final say on sketches, was hazardous.

If the committee chose two or three different designs, which they directed to be merged together, the result ended up being something of a camel (a horse designed by a committee!)

I felt very strongly that the only things that should be shown to the committee were properties that echoed the final product, a model made out of some hard material that could be properly painted and chromed.

A fully finished model with a see-through top is the only thing that should be presented, and should form the basis of the committee's judgement.

It does not require a feat of imagination to understand and this process makes for a smoother progress in the approval phase. The committee is unlikely to make whimsical changes to the model if it is in such a finished state, rather than knowing that it can be easily changed. I proposed that no sketches, unless they were there to support some particular detail, should be shown to the committee.

The reason for this is that these early sketches are often little more than caricatures that need considerable interpretation by those who have the expertise to do so. This was generally becoming an accepted practice in the business and Harold accepted that approach.

Our new procedure was that we had the usual briefing given to the designers, something I did after discussing with Product Planning and all other areas where the general direction of the model would go. All of this information was given to my people in a briefing, and they were pointed in that particular direction after internal discussions. That ensured the cohesion of the model range could be maintained.

Selected sketches were made to go to full-sized clays, which were viewed within the design office, and the final selections made then, maybe one or two designs were finished off in fibreglass with a see-through top; and this was what was presented to the committee. If it was turned down, that would cause a major timing glitch, but in my experience that rarely happened if done this way.

In the end, we finished up with a collection of fibreglass models because the first ones were for basic selection, then there would be an interim one, then a final model, which would be kept for reference. This was the master model and if there was any major deviation in process after this stage then we had something to refer back to that had been previously approved.

That was the process we followed and with this, plus the integrity of the computer data and the staff training in other areas, we felt that the end result would be of a very much higher quality. Clearly with the arrival of the first car to go through this process, the Rover 800, the potential was not realised.

Regrettably the accuracy issues were not resolved properly by this method, and it was difficult to see how deviations had taken place. Some vital element here was missing, but that did not come to light until some time around the end of Harold's time. Andy Barr, the manufacturing director had taken a very key role in pushing all this along, but it still failed to reach its objectives.

This was a major disappointment all round, and was really the cause of the catastrophe in the American market when the Sterling (nee 800) was launched.

In the run-up to Rover 800 production, an agreement was struck between AR and a prominent dealer in Florida to market the Rover 800 in the USA. That was a very key element of the whole Rover 800 idea, the return to the USA. This would boost production volumes considerably and make a big difference to what could be achieved in new product in the UK.

There was a lot of emphasis in the plan that this car would be produced to new high quality levels which was the biggest concern that the American team had, having seen people burn their fingers before with British cars. A great deal of effort was put into convincing the Americans that this quality standard was going to be met.

Norman Braman was the name of the multi-millionaire dealer who formed the company ARCONA in the USA and set it all up to sell Sterlings (they didn't want to try and revive the Rover name in the USA for a third time). I had spent a lot of time with Norman and his key man Ray Ketridge, being quizzed constantly as to whether this car really would meet the promised standards.

I did my best to reassure them that I believed that, to the best of my ability to assess the situation, what was being done in the plants and by engineering was enough to ensure we met the quality standards required.

Many Rover 800 Coupé proposals were shown, and gradually became more conservative as the project went on.

Norman and his team were always very happy with the appearance of the Rover 800, and in dealer and press presentations the car went down extremely well. They liked the look of it and the market research that was done backed this up, not that I put great store in the opinions of market researchers. Nevertheless the car never offended anyone, and many were really enthused subject to those quality promises.

When the car reached production, the quality goal was not realised. A huge amount of money and effort had been expended but manufacturing and engineering failed to deliver.

The result was that the car very quickly got a bad reputation for fit and finish, and a myriad of other problems, causing a complete disaster in the end with all the old chestnuts regarding British cars being voiced.

Finally, the only thing to do was to withdraw from that market completely, a story for later.

What the Americans told me from day one, was what they really wanted was a two-door coupé. But in the end, they had to settle for the four-door because there was no money and it was felt that the four-door had to prove itself before the two-door could follow.

This type of vehicle was not very popular in the UK and Europe, and the feeling was that another alternative, possibly a five-door, which the Americans had no interest in, would be a better use of limited resources.

However, we had produced the CCV, and the Americans could not understand why they couldn't have that right away.

A compromise was brought about, though with the UK view prevailing. The Rover SD1 was a hatchback, and although we deliberately went with the saloon format for the 800, the hatchback was a reasonable proposition for European markets and could be made into a sportier looking car.

Would this 800-based convertible have sold in the USA?

We, in design, devised a fastback that carried over the rear as well as the front doors from the saloon, and this was quite an accomplishment, not often achieved, and big financial savings were possible.

The Americans accepted this position as better than only being offered the saloon. We were quite happy with what we had with this fastback design. Whether it was necessary or not, who knows, or whether the model would have survived just as well without it?

Nevertheless, it offered another dimension to the range. At no time was an estate version ever considered.

The Americans wanted a lot more wood inside the car, but the people in the UK were appalled at the prospect, as wood inside cars was getting a bad reception at the time. And I must admit I blanched at where the Americans were suggesting so much wood, for example, the background to the instruments, the steering wheel and as much wood as you could pile in. They were right though, as most luxury cars sold today in the USA are equipped this way!

They couldn't have their way anyway, as most of these parts had already been tooled, and it was not possible to incorporate a wood overlay on these parts, so maybe we were saved from the worst excesses of this direction. In any case, I don't think it would have made a difference, one way or the other as what killed the Sterling, in my admittedly biased opinion, was certainly not the appearance.

Much was made about the shared parts between the Honda and Rover and although the Honda didn't look as good to some people, there was no doubt about the built quality, something Rover totally failed to achieve. It was altogether a sorry tale, and one, which I fear really finally finished British cars in the USA.

The plan was that the new designs would be clearly defined visually as Rover and Honda, and the hope was that this formula, with the possible exception of the Metro sized vehicle, would be on a common base with a Honda model for the relative size of vehicle. The interiors and exteriors would be unique to each company, a plan agreed to by Honda.

When the plan was complete we produced mock-up fibreglass models of the full future projected range of vehicles, and placed them in the showroom of the design offices giving us the chance to see the full range and what the future held in store. This was particularly useful for showing to government representatives, who were forever hovering around trying to give us the benefit of their wisdom.

When I joined the company, Product Planning was playing an increasingly strong hand, and looked like taking over the direction in which the design office could go, even commissioning designs from outside the company without in-house design office participation.

Other departments were also pulling in their own directions, hence the myriad of conflicting ideas. In fairness this was being done out of exasperation with in-house design. Product Planning was bringing in outside design help, particularly from Italy, and I'd had experience of this situation before, at Chrysler where this occasionally happened.

I've nothing but admiration for the Italian coach building industry. They've inspired me on many occasions, and continue to do so, but what they had a bad habit of doing, at that time, was selling a basic design to more than one company.

This can easily be seen when looking at the offerings of Peugeot, BL and other companies in the '60s. It was the time of grilles, so each marque could be given its own frontal identity, but overall, the same basic design was offered to different companies. Very often, too, the production cars fell well short of the glamorous models produced for motor shows where no feasibility restrictions applied. The Italians couldn't do any better than the in-house team, if the in house people were given the same terms of reference as I think we demonstrated with EX-E and CCV.

Unfortunately, an in-house design frequently shown and re-shown so many times to committees would end up being worked over so many times that company executives would become familiar to the point of boredom. When an outside designer was brought in with a new design without such interference, it was like a breath of fresh air but unlikely to meet the design brief for dimensions or in some other way.

If the design was chosen, it was left for the long-suffering in-house design team to bring it into line often resulting in a very unsatisfactory result for which the in-house team got the blame. It was a no win situation and very frustrating.

This was bad practice, and very demoralising for the in-house design team of designers, to see a car approved that they did not create but had to make into a practical proposition. This was a practice I put an immediate stop to. We did go outside and ask for assistance, as there were times when it was fortuitous and necessary to do so to get input from an outside design house. At other times this was done to use their expertise to produce things in prototype form that we were unable to do in-house. This was done with proper controls and often proved very supportive.

As for our new design team, as far as the MG EX-E, the CCV and other products that were produced, particularly those that never saw the light of day, our designs did underscore the fact that the personnel objectives had been achieved. In other words, the task to put a professional team of people together inside three years, with I might add, the good fortune of taking on the staff that Peugeot abandoned in the UK, was completed successfully.

I had a considerable amount of satisfaction later on, to see that same group under BMW, and later the Ford Motor Company, at Gaydon in an all-new building, continuing to produce designs to very high professional standards. I had a great deal of satisfaction in what was achieved in those first three or four years working with Harold Musgrove.

The overall accomplishment in design in the four and a half years between my joining AR and Harold's departure were considerable and a credit to the team. The aim to produce a really first rate design operation was achieved. A whole range of cars for AR was designed including two show cars, which I am proud of, and which showed the capabilities of our designers if allowed to work without interference.

There was also the relationship with Honda, which was established on a very sound and lasting relationship between the design departments of the two companies.

The Rover 800 was designed and put into production, and the vehicle I have not talked about yet, the R8 (later the 200/400), which was also a joint venture with Honda, but which turned into something that was not expected.

R8 definitely was a case a right first time ...

The formula for following the idea of a unique body shell based upon common underpinnings fell by the wayside as a result of a lack of money and resources on the part of AR.

Part of the resource problem, largely in engineering, was caused through the continuing problems with Maestro, Montego and Metro, and then finally, with Rover 800.

The 800 overran the design phase and absorbed a tremendous amount of effort in trying to resolve the quality problems on the prototype cars as production approached.

The design of the intermediate sized cars, to replace the Maestro and Montego, which were designated AR16 & AR17, as well as the AR6, which was Metro sized, dropped by the wayside because of all the effort being concentrated on the 800 programme.

Financial problems crept in at this point causing a change of tack, which was to try and introduce a smaller vehicle in below the Rover 800, a joint product with Honda. The whole of the centre portion of the AR and Honda vehicles would be common, the differences being confined to bumpers and grilles and a limited amount of front and rear end sheet metal, which were low cost and simple to do.

This was just a step up on the Triumph Acclaim but deemed better than nothing, and it did have the advantage that, as no design existed at Honda yet, the two design departments could develop the design to suit both partners' requirements. So, we embarked on the R8 programme.

This project put the two design office teams into a parallel situation, as distinct from the competitive situation with the Rover 800 and Honda Legend. What we had to do was get an agreement between the two design groups as to what was an acceptable joint exterior for this vehicle in the common areas, yet which still enabled sufficient work to be done by each team to make it clear that the two cars' identities were quite separate.

The final part of the design work was all done in Japan. Obviously we first did our two dimensional design work in England producing a set of ideas we could work from but because the car was going to rely heavily on Honda's engineering, it was necessary to move our team to Japan in order to work with the Japanese studio. A special studio in the Tokyo offices was set up to do this.

This way of working taxed the relationship between the two design teams, but in the end, things worked relatively smoothly. We both had a similar idea of what this vehicle should look like, and we were down to the detail of how the window areas and belt line treatments should be done when it came down to making final decisions on the vehicle itself.

All of this was done between the teams at Rover and Honda, which were located in the same studio in Tokyo with very little involvement by the senior members of the company. Our team had to go out there and camp out, as it were, for a few months. This was a considerable strain for some, because they were away from home for a long period of time.

The Honda team had other members from their main studios who came in from time to time and it was intriguing for us to see new faces arriving all the time. The team that came to the UK on the Rover 800 was under the leadership of Iwakura-san, who was my equivalent in Honda. His right hand man on the 800 project was 'Ted' Misuno who to us seemed more like a design administrator than a designer, but he was the man who really helped out on that project and was a good English speaker. He later became the head of the Honda studios in Germany, and my son Chris worked for him there for a couple of years.

When we went to the design studios in Japan on the R8 programme, Ted, who had been with the Honda team on the XX programme, was about to move to Germany. There was another person, Zima, who came in and out a lot just to view the model. He didn't speak any English at all at the time, but was conferring with Iwakura, and he was obviously passing comments on the cars to him so it was obvious to us, he was pretty senior.

At no time did we ever see any real organizational or structural chart to say who was who in the Honda hierarchy. So we didn't know who was who or even how many studios Honda had, and this was not clarified until much later on. I remember one incident when we were trying to resolve one of the last difficult areas of the car, which concerned the doors at the rear quarter panels and the flow through of the belt line.

Iwakura and I were discussing it at length, and each made proposals; and in the final model, these two proposals were put together one on each side of the model. Ours had a straighter line, and Honda's kicked up on the rear part of the rear door. Zima san came in and starting making comments in Japanese to Iwakura, and at one point, I stepped forward to Iwakura and asked, 'Zima-san has looked at our designs a few times, what are his opinions on the two alternative solutions?'

Iwakura replied, 'Axe-san, Zima works for me, and has no opinion,' which was intriguing! I think what was really being said was that whatever opinions the Honda designers had, they would be voiced through Iwakura, whose opinion was the final word and what he said went. Interestingly Zima went on to head the Tokyo styling offices after Iwakura was promoted, and I would have a lot to do with him in later years when we were doing consulting work for Honda.

The R8 went through smoothly. Honda did all the body engineering, after the Rover engineers decided that they could not handle the workload. As far as we were concerned, we then had only one engineering team to deal with and this cut out many drawn out situations where the two engineering teams had to resolve their differences.

The R8 eventually went into production as a five-door car, and then models unique to Rover followed on. After that there was the two-door, and then the four-door version of the car, which had a boot. These models were very successful for Rover in England. I have a rule of thumb as to which cars in a range are likely to be successful; they are never the most dramatic, expensive or sporting, because by nature those types are low volume. The really successful ones are really well done middle of the road models in the Ford Escort class for example. A successful design in this category brings success to the company's bottom line almost without exception, because this is the sought-after combination of high volume and high margin because of demand.

Rover had very good sales out of the R8, it was well liked by customers, and quality levels were much higher than they had been in the past. Of course, a design that does not have a dramatic look in this category will have a relatively short life in the marketplace, and a regular replacement plan is required. This was something that ARG and BL before it did not really understand but Honda did.

There were many tedious meetings on the subject of trying to cram the issue of quality into everyone during this period. Harold ran long meetings trying to do this and his intentions were the very best. He was dedicated to trying to sort this out, and he firmly believed that the way he was trying to approach this would achieve these aims.

I think Honda was amazed at the situation at Rover regarding engineering and manufacturing. On one occasion, two senior people from Honda took me out to lunch in Tokyo, and were talking about this very issue. They said they could not understand why I worked for a company that worked this way, and this was a depressing thing to be told, however, I believe Honda was genuinely willing to offer help in this regard. The Japanese had mastered the issue of quality, and for anyone who doubts it try owning a Honda for a while. Honda and Toyota are on top of the pile in terms of quality and reliability particularly with their premium brands, Acura (Honda) and Lexus (Toyota).

Honda wanted to stretch out a hand and help with the quality issues, if only they had been invited. They were not in a position to do much without invitation, however, they knew how Rover built its cars because they came into the plants and were shown around. We were shown around their plants but not everything. If we had humbled ourselves, and asked Honda for help, I believe they would have done so and Rover's cars would have improved in quality hand over fist.

In the end, that is exactly what Honda was invited to do but much later, with cars such as the R8 and the 600-series. These were much better than the Rover 800, and were largely engineered by Honda, but the damage had already been done. Honda just could not understand the Maestro and the Montego, they just failed to understand how anyone could turn out products like that.

When we presented the R8, we did so as joint Honda and Rover projects, and to both company managements at the same time. The senior management from Rover had all travelled from the UK for the final approval meeting, and we all sat around a large table in front of the models which were finally signed off by both sides.

Mr Kumo, who was in charge of Honda was a rather stocky, quiet, but very shrewd guy, who would often just sit in on the activities in design at any time of the day. On this occasion, Harold was feeling extremely feisty, and was pounding the table insisting that this car, for which Honda had full responsibility for engineering, should be built with the quality commensurate for this kind of car, which I thought was an incredible cheek! I just couldn't imagine anyone would do that, but Harold had this burning determination that this thing was eventually going to get right. The Japanese just took this in their stride.

One amusing thing that happened at another meeting: Joe Farnham had decided that he would come out to Japan a day earlier to join this big meeting regarding the R8. He did not do well with jetlag and he needed time to get over this. We followed the next day, arriving in Japan in the afternoon, with the meeting in the following morning. We had got used to this commuting by then; I did the trip very many times, often for a one or two day meeting, and it was a long trip! We were able to travel in comfort, so that was half the battle.

At the time of the R8 work I was commuting once every three weeks. We arrived at our hotel, sitting in the foyer, after getting ourselves checked-in, when I asked where Joe was. I was told that Joe had arrived and that he would be with us shortly. Joe arrived in the reception area propped up by two people, after tripping over something in the garden near to the hotel, damaging his leg.

This was a major disaster in the making, and we all ended up going to our rooms as Joe limped away. The following morning, he was in considerable pain with his leg but we got him into the car, which had come to collect us. Joe sat in the back with his leg virtually out of the window because he couldn't bend it. We arrived at the meeting and needless to say, everyone felt great sympathy for Joe apart from Harold, who felt he'd done something he should not have done! The Japanese were all concerned about Joe, and rather than have him attend the meeting, they whisked him away to the local hospital to have him checked out.

Joe arrived back at the meeting, which was still in session, with his foot in a large cast, and stated that he had fractured a bone in his leg, and really needed to get back to the UK as soon as he could.

Joe felt that he was pretty useless attending a meeting in that state, but Harold didn't see it that way. The meeting had been completed with regard to the styling issues by then, and it had gone extremely well; we knew what we were doing and everything was in good shape. I had no problems leaving Gordon Sked behind to clear up a few details while I went back to the UK to do other things, so I volunteered to escort Joe back to the UK. We were put on a first class flight back to the UK, and after we boarded, he settled in and ordered himself a large Scotch, and we took off.

After a couple of these Scotches, Joe was starting to complain that his foot was starting to hurt quite a bit, and I could see his toes going blue out of the end of this cast; obviously the whisky wasn't doing much good, so in the end we had to get the engineer from the flight deck to come back. He got his tool kit out, and cut away a little bit of Joe's cast to relieve the pressure on his foot, and we were eventually able to make it to Anchorage (in the days before we could fly over Russia).

We got out of the plane there, I got Joe into a wheelchair, and I wheeled him around the airport for the hour while we were on the ground. We then loaded him back onboard, and Joe said he felt a lot better and immediately ordered another Scotch. We then went through the same thing again on the flight from Anchorage to London.

I was exhausted by the time we got to Heathrow. I got him off the plane, wheeled him through customs, and his chauffeur, Arthur, was there to meet him. He got Joe onto the back seat with the front seat folded down, so he could get his leg up and was whisked away. I was met by my driver and taken home in a totally exhausted state. And that was that.

The following morning, I went into the office, and was behind my desk mid way through the morning, when the door opened, and in walked Joe. I said, 'What are you doing here, what are you doing on your feet like this?' Joe said he got home, and his wife was worried about him, and took him to the hospital and they'd done another X-ray, and decided that there was nothing seriously wrong with his foot at all, had taken the cast off and let him go home. So there he was in my office. I was speechless!

The problems with the Montego, Maestro and Metro would never go away. They were inherent in the design right from the beginning; the quality was not built in, the very expensive robotic production systems just hadn't worked, and I just had the feeling all along that the company was being used as a test bed for these computer systems.

The end result was that none of this technology delivered what it should have. There were all kinds of people involved and they were levelled with all kinds of blame, but the problem was that all of this technology did not deliver quality and reliability as promised and the company was just nailed to the wall with warranty costs and the resulting poor customer relationships.

So this great future we'd been looking at in the very early 1980s when we felt this would all be delivered never materialised. That was the root of all the problems that were to follow in the Rover Company because it was the time Harold left and the end of the road in terms of being able to recoup reputations and put the thing back on track.

In the final days before the arrival of the new regime, there was activity to try to replace the Metro and the Maestro/Montego with new product. A lot of work went into this at the design stage, and fibreglass models were made in order to view the potential of the new range but the finances were not there.

I was unhappy with subsequent proposals to rebody the Maestro/Montego as I felt that proportionally, these cars were becoming dated with the front wheels being so far back. We did try some partial re-skin ideas to round off the body features, but this proved to be an expensive way to make a marginal improvement.

Harold made a short-lived reorganisation, placing Mark Snowdon as a sort of product development boss, to whom both Joe Farnham and I reported. Neither Joe nor I were happy with this, but that was the way Harold wanted it.

I was given an increase in responsibility, adding advanced engineering to my operation. This transferred a number of engineers into my studio, and gave me the opportunity to develop new ideas though this was restricted by financial restraints.

Mike Pendry was appointed to run advanced engineering, and we went ahead with a project to produce a new small car (codenamed R6X) using as many existing components as we could.

Engineering had no capacity to build a prototype so I turned to Sergio Coggiola, who had has own company producing prototypes in Italy. He wasn't really a styling house; his expertise was producing prototypes for other people. He was quick, but would also turn out a nice piece of work.

I had met Sergio years before when he was at Ghia when it was an independent, and they'd been doing a lot of work for Chrysler. Sergio was an extremely nice man with a very 'can do' approach. He would do things which from a business point of view he really shouldn't have done, but he put his heart and soul into everything he did.

He took on the build of this design, which was delivered back to us as a fully running prototype. The exterior was done with involvement from people like Dave Saddington and Richard Woolley, two very talented designers, and Graham Lewis and his people put together an interior design for it.

It was produced in Italy with supervision from them and with body engineering from Mike Pendry and his team. Everyone was impressed by the car; it was good looking and would have been competitive in the marketplace, and I think pretty successful had it been built, but even that was beyond the scope of anyone being able to cope with from within ARG. Coggiola was extremely proud of what he'd achieved, but there was no follow on for him regrettably and even more sadly, Sergio died at quite an early age not long after that.

Engineering, on the basis of not-invented-here, was not really supportive, but it did not have the resources anyway due to redesign work that it was doing just to get out of the warranty mess.

When I joined Rover, Norman Morris was the only engineer who reported to Design, and even that had been recent as Joe Farnham felt, when he joined the company, that such an engineering person was needed for liaison. Norman had no real clout but he did try.

When the new premises at Canley were ready we increased the staff in this area, bringing in Geoff Hurley from Peugeot (a member of my old team there) together with some good people to help out in this important area. Graham LeCornu was the ace computer man, and stayed with me after the Rover era. When advanced engineering was added to my responsibility, Mike Pendry took over. He was a quiet pipe-smoking engineer with a great 'can do' attitude, and his work was greatly appreciated.

During this period, a whole range of cars had been designed, but financially we were at a standstill. The company was getting no support from the government, which saw Rover as a case of good money following bad. All these designs were stillborn when the change of management came, following Harold's departure, and that change did not bring about new finance either. The Rover 800 facelift was the only new project to go ahead.

18

The Rover Group and the Graham Day Era: 1986–1988

ANY GOVERNMENT WOULD HAVE struggled to finance an industrial concern such as BL, so perhaps the fact that it wanted out was actually good news. But who would want to come in? That was the really difficult thing. Harold Musgrove, who had done his very best and bent over backwards to get this ship to sail, failed to do so because he was let down by various parts of the operation and the end result was that the government simply lost patience with the whole thing. Westminster decided to try something else and so, on one fateful day, it was announced that a new appointment was to be made, that there would be someone new to run the company, and with it came a big reorganization.

Graham Day, the man chosen, was a person from outside the car industry. He was a kind of industry doctor/trouble-shooter, and had been on assignment in the ship building yards to try and resolve their problems for the government and now he was being brought in to solve BL's problems and if possible, to dispose of the company into the private sector. Harold Musgrove at this point resigned, as did Mark Snowdon and a number of other people. It was quite a big tear-up and déjà-vu for me!

Graham Day was a Canadian and with his black hair and beard, he cut a rather formidable figure. In person, however, he was quite affable, and I have to say that he was always very supportive of our work in Design. When Graham arrived he renamed BL 'The Rover Group', creating a new company image, with a whole new board of directors.

The new MD was Les Wharton, someone who I would be closely associated with as time went by, but whom few of us knew. He came in from the old Leyland Truck operation, and had the reputation of being a very tough man in terms of being able to cut costs and waste and he proved to be up to that task.

A number of other new people came in, there were changes to the finance and sales departments, and whole areas of the company were changed. The Engineering department under Joe Farnham and the Design department under me both remained much as they were, and we became members of the board of the new company.

Throughout my time working with Graham Day he was always supportive of what we were doing, perhaps it was helpful to him that we were the only department in the company that really had all the mock-ups and models. They could be put together to show to the government and explain to would-be purchasers of the company what the potential was at that time. Again, this was déjà-vu for me, back to the Iacocca era at Chrysler!

We, in design, were, I believe, quite useful to Graham in that period of time. He was a somewhat aloof individual, in the sense that we didn't see him too much, and he was based in London. Les Wharton told me in later years that, although he was the Managing Director and Graham was the Chairman, he hardly saw Graham at all. He was given a free hand to try and 'knock some sense' (as Les used to say) into the Rover Group.

Les was a no-nonsense Lancashire man who was very canny at finance. He did not stand any nonsense at all, and while he did not have a detailed understanding of the car business, he was very good at finding all the waste within the company, and a very quick learner and fixer. He only remained as MD for a couple of years, but during that period, he made tremendous inroads into cutting overheads and for a short period, Rover did get back on its feet again.

This was to be a very frustrating time, and it was really mentally fatiguing to me. I had experienced this before, but there's only so many times you can go around the cycle before you feel, hey, we have to do something different here. The sales department was also doing its best with what it had, but people were dropping by the wayside too. Kevin Morley was brought in and quickly took over the whole of Sales and Marketing, and he was very much under the wing of Graham Day.

There were some good people in the sales department dropping out: Peter Johnson who was a very good guy and very much a supporter of the American Sterling concept even if that was becoming radically out of favour by both sides, called it a day; as did Norman Braman, who had taken on the task to market the Sterling in the USA, and who had set up the full organization. He was becoming very frustrated with the very poor quality cars that were coming through; the thing that he feared the most before the launch was now actually happening.

Back at home everyone was getting frustrated with the American operation for not performing with sales; it was a catch-22 situation. Attempts had been made to find a way to build a coupé version of the Rover 800. In the latter months of ARG, Mark Snowdon felt that we should see if there was a way by using the coupé building expertise in Italy, and both Pininfarina and Bertone had this capability.

Mark arranged a viewing of proposals we had done at Canley, as well as some produced by Bertone. This was something of a surprise to us, as our proposals based on the CCV show car had been very well received by everyone. At the viewing I think everyone, except perhaps Mark Snowdon, was confused. Certainly Signore Bertone was unclear and asked me what was happening, and I had no good answer for him. After a rather embarrassing couple of hours, it was decided to use our model of the car as the design and for Bertone to work out the feasibility of the design for production with a view to manufacture in his plant. This idea was pursued for some time before being finally dropped.

After the 'Palace Revolution', it was decided to try again. As the car was really for the USA market, I suggested that we try a venture with American Sunroof, a very experienced company that I had been familiar with when at Chrysler. Heinz Prekter was the company founder, and was someone I knew quite well, but he was no longer in the day-to-day operations at that time. He was a very well respected businessman right up to the White House level, and ran a very good company.

The idea then was to use as many of the Rover 800 parts as we could, but try to achieve as close a look to the CCV as possible. Though all sides tried very hard to do this, it was not successful. I had sent a promising young designer, Adrian Griffiths, over to the USA for a time to handle the project for us. He did a fine job, but the design was a backward step from the CCV because of the carry-over from the 800, and it was eventually abandoned. I think the compromises were way too much in the end, and the car would not have worked well in that form had it gone ahead.

A final effort was made much later as I was leaving the company. This was a coupé that can best be described as a two-door saloon as it was literally that in style and content. Richard Woolley and David Saddington were again involved and though they did a nice job by then the USA was out of the picture, and the base design was getting very old. Overall the effort was not worth it by then, but the car did see limited production.

The situation regarding the catastrophic quality problems in the USA came to a head. Les Wharton was charged by Graham Day to go over to Florida and terminate the agreement, and this he duly did. He went over to Miami and there was a final meeting, which resulted in the company being closed, or more accurately Norman Braman being bought-out so that it could be closed.

Les said later that he was very upset during the meeting, as Norman Braman needed some decision from him, and he was unable to make it without referring back to base. Norman said he, Norman, didn't have to refer back to anyone because the big difference between him and Les was that he, Norman Braman, was the man in charge and the owner of his business, and could make his own decisions, whereas Les should remember that even though he had the grand title of MD, he was only a paid employee!

That cut poor old Les to the quick, and he never forgot it, but nevertheless it was the truth. That was the sad and expensive ending to the mishandled US operation and I have to say that while it wasn't perfect from the American side, they were given a very bad hand in terms of the quality of the cars that were sent over. There were some horrendous problems with those vehicles in the American climactic conditions that should have been foreseen. It was all a very frustrating exercise and Sterling had a similar fate to that of French and Italian cars in the USA for the same basic reasons.

19

Rover Group and BAe: 1988–1992

To EVERYONE'S SURPRISE, it was announced one day that a deal had been struck between Graham Day (on behalf of the British Government) and Roland Smith (the Chairman of British Aerospace, BAe). Basically, BAe would takeover Rover by buying out the government's stake in the company for £800m.

This was out of the blue to most people and a big surprise. Synergy between the two companies was something that was stressed, but there really was not any. It became obvious that no significant new car was going to be financed, as BAe certainly wasn't going to back any expensive projects like that. In fact, BAe approved very little during the time it was in charge. It simply sold off a few assets, which covered the original purchase of Rover, and was quite clearly preparing for the chance to sell Rover. I firmly believed that they already believed they had a buyer in the form of Honda but they got a surprise at the end of the day!

After Graham Day took over, Marketing was getting stronger by the day. He was really a marketing man, and so was Roland Smith. It was between the pair that the merger had taken place, and this placed Kevin Morley in a very strong position and he quickly replaced Trevor Taylor as director of sales and marketing.

Kevin was a bombastic, go ahead, ambitious young guy, but he was not only very strong in marketing, but now also ran the sales department, too. Not an easy man to get on with, and I had a couple of good showdowns with him but nevertheless that's life. Overall we tolerated each other, and ended up getting on reasonably well.

He was pushing for improvements in the model line; bigger wheels, all these kinds of things which I couldn't argue with, as I wanted them too. Engineering had traditionally resisted these changes, which we had not managed to achieve, so to give Kevin his due, he pushed through some things that I'd failed to do. In that sense, he was doing as much as he could, making the best out of a bad job and could be considered an ally of the design department in that regard.

As a result of the problems with the 800, there was a need to do something with it. The Americans had continually badgered for the car to gain a stronger, more traditional identity, something that made it seem more 'British'. What's wrong with a grille for example?

Well, what was wrong at the time the 800 was originally designed, was that due to the Vanden Plas Allegro connotations, grilles were definitely not the in thing in Austin-Rover. Anyone who suggested the original car should have had a grille on it would have been ridiculed. However, times had changed and there was pressure from the USA, plus new marketing people in the company. It also helped that grilles were starting to re-appear in other companies in response to lack of frontal identity, and that made the time right to put a grille back on the front of a Rover.

Obviously any grille we used needed to have as much Rover character as possible, but be applied in the lowest cost way possible. So we changed only as much of the surrounding metal as was needed. The plan was that the middle of the car would remain the same, although it did call for a complete retool for the door area because of the poor sealing and other problems.

The work involved engineering an all-new design of door, but this was too much for engineering, so the original design was carried over with modifications. However, despite these doors being retooled, it didn't solve the problem at all, because the mating panel on the inner panel for door sealing was not changed, and the retooled doors were little better from a fit and finish standpoint than the old ones. We had the totally frustrating situation where the chance to change the whole middle section of the car – or rather I should say, the whole side section of the car running all the way front to rear (as the doors' outer section dictated this with their feature lines), had been lost.

If you have a car intended to be around six years, and you keep it going for 12, then you're going to be running into a different design philosophy era and substantial changes are needed. But this was as far as the company would go to refresh the design, back to the old BL ways! The chance to update the Rover 800 at the same cost as had been expended anyway replacing the doors with ones of the same design was wasted.

That was a tragic lost opportunity. At the rear of the car, we felt that boot height in comparison with the competition was low, and by raising it, we had a chance of softening the form. Combined with the more rounded front and rear end, we had the opportunity of giving the car a more impressive appearance to create a bigger looking and more updated look to the car. That was the route we took.

These ideas came from the design department, and that work was taken on to try and illustrate to Les Wharton, what changing these components could do to prolong the life of the 800. We built a model which incorporated all these things, and one evening I asked Les to come down and look at the current car alongside this new proposal, with its limited but nevertheless quite effective change.

Les was impressed enough that this became the proposal to update the 800. Richard Hamlin's advanced studio produced a model to show what a completely rebodied 800 would look like, illustrating that a step further would achieve an even better result, but the cost of doing this, I knew, was completely out of the question. All we could really do was push for the facelift, which did at least eke out the life of the Rover 800. Eventually it lasted more than twice the time it was designed to! This was nothing to be proud of though, as it should have been replaced long before that.

All of this was, once again, very much déjà vu as far as I was concerned; it all smacked of my years prior to the Iacocca era at Chrysler, when we were struggling with no investment money and trying to make silk purses out of sows' ears. That was what we were going through again, and I was getting extremely disillusioned during this period, and not at all happy with the way I could see things going.

I really couldn't see a good ending to it all. Something drastic was going to take place at some point, and I could not see BAe continuing with the company, although there was still a lot of talk bandied about concerning synergy and the way they could feed off each other in terms of technologies.

The way they made aircraft was completely different to cars, and you only had to go down to an aircraft plant and see what went on to be convinced of that. The people at

BAe had no expertise in the car industry, and they weren't very interested either, they had problems of their own!

Obviously that was not why that company had been bought; it had been purchased cheaply from the government for the opportunity of doing a very nice deal for the shareholders in passing the company on in some way later on. The plan that Graham Day and Roland Smith had put together to merge these companies continued until another turning point that occurred in 1989.

The previous year, John Towers joined the company and took over the engineering operations, and Joe Farnham retired. Although he seemed pleasant enough, I never really felt comfortable with John. I don't know why, but sometimes that kind of thing happens. Of course John was to gain some notoriety later on after he and his consortium purchased what became MG Rover from BMW, and which all ended in disaster and scandal.

Les Wharton had been about to turn a modest profit for the company, and although his successor actually took the credit for that, this was all down to Les. There were so many things in the company that were wasteful that had been custom and practice for far too long, and Les was able to root out a lot of it. He should have been basking in the glory of having finally got the company on an even keel, however, with the purchase of the Rover Group by BAe, subsequent events really caused another major upheaval, which took place in 1989.

That was when Graham Day announced to Les (in Les's words): 'Well, you've done a pretty good job Les, but now it's time for you to retire. We need to put in a younger man who can take this company on through the next ten years or so.' With that, Les was effectively dismissed, much to his total annoyance and disgust. He didn't totally leave the company, however, because after he was retired from the position of MD at Rover group, BAe used his considerable talents in and around their many companies doing the same thing for them that he'd just done for Rover as a company trouble-shooter!

His ability to root out old practices and systems that ate up the profitability of the companies was second to none. What was even more ironic was that the man to replace him was one of his protégés and this really made life rather difficult for Les. This was George Simpson, later Lord Simpson, who gained considerable infamy later on. He took over the company at that point and proceeded to make some quite drastic changes. A lot of those changes affected design and engineering and were instigated, I suspect, by John Towers.

In actual fact it was clear to me, that this situation was going to end up being very different from what I had originally joined the company to do, and to give them credit, I think the people at the top of the company realised that too. They told me that they were going to make these changes, and they didn't think what they had in mind would be very satisfactory to me, in that they were basically going to dilute the role of the design office for the future putting it under a product development umbrella with John Towers in charge.

The design department was going to take a lesser role, in fact returning to the old relationships at BL. This was going to put things back to how it was before I joined the company and I thought it was a completely retrograde step. This was explained to me and they were, of course, entitled to do what they felt they had to do and there was no argument from me. I was quite an old campaigner and I had already been thinking that I should do something else at this point.

I was given a proposition. It was explained to me that they didn't want to lose my position in terms of expertise within the company and for inputting ideas, in fact they wanted to enhance that situation. At the same time they knew that I was not disinterested in forming some kind of design consultancy. I guess I had been talking about this, and the word had got through.

Their idea was for me to set up a consultancy, and they would put a good contract my way both to get me established and also to take my ambition on further and satisfy the situation all round. I turned that down, because it did not seem to me that it was sensible to take that kind of risk in that kind of way. I wasn't quite sure where that was going to lead me as far as Rover was concerned.

After a short time, they came up with a revised proposal, which was to set up an operation in a separate location, which could be fully equipped to my requirements, to take on a staff, which I could choose from the staff I already had and that staff could return to Rover should they wish without any loss of benefits after two years.

Also, this organisation would be given a contract from the Rover Group, which could be a very firm base from which we could operate. That also included BAe, as we were starting to get involved in interior aircraft design work. This operation would be still owned by Rover, but could be taken over by me after two years and my relationship to the company would be as a consultant in effect.

I really couldn't go far wrong and the people that I had chosen to join me were safe as they were guaranteed positions back at Rover if they chose to leave me, so I accepted that approach in principle, and that was the beginnings of the formation of Design Research Associates initially as a subsidiary of the Rover Group. The location we chose was on the outskirts of Leamington Spa. All this boiled down to an offer one could not refuse, as they say.

On moving from my position with Rover, I recommended that Gordon Sked be my replacement, and this was accepted, and Gordon took charge. Not too long afterwards BMW, in a stunningly surprise move, bought Rover Group from BAe including Land Rover. Quite what BMW had been thinking remains a mystery. I always felt that BMW had perhaps been after Range Rover really, and that it expected to be able to sell the car division on to Honda. If so, it was in for a shock, and I could have told them that Honda would rather go its own way; the Japanese knew too much about Rover to want to own it and BMW knew too little!

Gordon Sked left the company a short time later and I lost touch with him.

20

The DRA/DRAL Era: 1992–1999

THE OTHER THING THAT I became involved with, as I have mentioned already, and before this organisational change, was the aircraft industry. Shortly before the BAe takeover of Rover, I had been having dinner with someone from that side of the business, and I suggested that we, as a design operation, had a lot to offer the aircraft side.

The lady I was speaking to was interested in this idea, and put me in touch with people from the executive aircraft side of the business, and so a relationship developed and became a very interesting additional direction to apply our design talents to. We would have liked to be more involved than we were, but it was a new direction and it did lead to other work outside BAe.

We had a couple of designers, Ian Beech and Graham Lewis, who were good at producing a full working drawing of the kind needed in this full-sized aircraft construction work. BAe gave us an introduction to both working directly for the company and with their subcontractors, who were making interiors for other companies as well as BAe.

The situation was very interesting and we started out with the project that BAe was about to introduce, the new 1000 series of its 125 jet. This was a new long distance version of the plane, which was longer than the original model, and we did two things for them: we did the external livery, and then we did a very nice interior as their demonstrator also showing how the useable interior space could be enlarged by some ergonomic work. During this time, the change to Design Research Associates Ltd, (DRA), an independent company, took place, and BAe continued to work with us.

The BAe 125 1000 demonstrator was very successful in a couple of ways: firstly, BAe liked the graphic so much on the exterior of the plane it used it as a theme logo and this was applied to all of its hangars, equipment and brochures. It was also a project that went on to production and it was therefore available to us for our own brochures. I believe about eight of these planes were built with the interior we designed, so we were pleased with that, and it did enable us to have some work that we could actually show to prospective clients. If the design had been for a private customer, this would likely not be the case, as customers generally wanted these things to remain confidential.

In this case, we were able to use pictures of the interior in various brochures for publicity purposes, not only for BAe, but also for Hunting who built the interior of the aircraft and ourselves. Exposure and publicity of this kind were very valuable to us, because so much of the work we did, at this time, was restricted by confidentiality agreements. When someone came to us and asked us to show what we could do, it was sometimes quite difficult to produce examples of the kinds of work our customers were asking for.

Aircraft interiors were a welcome addition to DRA's portfolio

The BAe work resulted in some production aircraft work, notably the SAAB 340 Generation 3. We also did a number of refurbished planes for BAe in the USA, the work being done on those aircraft in Atlanta Georgia and Chris Milburn led the project on site over there. These aeroplanes were converted and upgraded small turboprop airliners for use by some of the larger companies in the USA to ferry customers to various events. We did some interesting and sometimes spectacular VIP aircraft for heads of state too which can't be publicised unfortunately but the work included customers from across the world.

Later on as DRAL developed as a company, we were interested in getting into the design of large boats and yachts. We did some work, but we were limited to getting into the boat business through lack of experience and contacts on our part. However, the work we did was useful in being able to again publicise our design skills in various areas.

We also did other work, some associated with trains. I would have liked to move into product design, too, and although we had the capability, we didn't have enough expertise in the field. We were up against the consultancies that specialised in nothing else, and so it was a very difficult market to break into. Interestingly the product design people were interested in getting into automotive design but did not make too much progress, again due to lack of experience in the field! We did some work, for example, in the motorcycle industry and we did consider some specialised hiring to form a group to do product work but in the end, we gave up on that as we had plenty of work in the core areas we were familiar with.

DRA evolved into DRAL (Design Research Associates Ltd) after two years. Originally, as DRA been a department of Rover Group, we had been looking into future opportunities, and as such we were working exclusively on Rover and BAe projects.

We produced a luxury sports car project, numerous smaller projects and a replacement proposal for the Rover 800. When we were still DRA, Peter Ward, then Chairman of Rolls-Royce Motors, approached me with a view to doing work on new projects for his company. I explained that we were actually still Rover owned, and not an independent consultancy, but he still wanted our input. He asked me to talk to George Simpson to ask if this could be done, as RR and Rover were hardly competitors! I talked with George who readily agreed, and so we embarked on a relationship with RR, which continued until I retired.

At the end of our two years exclusive to Rover, we formed a separate company with the existing staff who all agreed to stay with us. DRAL was created, and Les Wharton, now not involved with Rover, joined us at my invitation as Chairman, which was a part time post.

I had formed a great respect for Les and his financial acumen and felt that this was an area where most designers need help! Les agreed to join us as a partner, and add the work to his other position as chairman of a trucks parts company. Two other directors were appointed, Adrian Griffiths and Graham Lewis, to take care of Exterior and Interior design respectively, and this team stayed in place until the company was sold at the end of 1999. Just before the sale, however Les died from an illness that had suddenly developed over a few short months. This was a great shock and a big loss to us. Les had been a good colleague and a good friend.

The ex-Rover staff stayed with DRAL and we had quite a few years with no staff changes as we embarked on a path that resulted in working for most of the world's car companies as well as many other interesting organizations and individuals outside the automobile industry. The Rolls-Royce work also developed into a very close relationship, and was a happy working experience too.

Peter Ward's right hand man on development was Mike Donovan, who we also developed an excellent relationship with. Mike moved on to run the BAe aircraft manufacturing plant near Manchester that made the BAe 146 Regional Jet four-engined regional airliner, which was used as a VIP jet. The relationship with Mike carried over, and we worked together on these projects for some time.

The relationship with Honda continued as well. After the separation from Rover, we worked closely with Honda again right through to my retirement, and my excellent relationship with Iwakura-san continued. Once again, due to confidentiality and the type of work we did for Honda, I am not able to illustrate the exciting projects that we worked on.

It is very difficult to be too specific about the work of the DRAL completed over the next nine years for a wide range of clients. The projects were extremely varied, and all of us involved found new experiences in different parts of the global market place and new experiences in the automotive business, because we had the opportunity of working with so many different companies.

This was the most interesting period in my career for me. Our main work was still cars, for companies in Japan, South Korea, England, France, Germany, Italy, and the USA. It was a true global experience.

It was all particularly interesting because it consisted of everything from 2D sketch work of ideas, some companies wanted just to feed into their own output, but increasingly, work on producing full-sized fibreglass models with interiors. These were models that we felt were a valid direction for companies who hired us to move towards. They could receive the models and evaluate what parts to use if any, or whether they wanted to use the whole thing. This work was also interesting in terms of relationships with larger companies who had different philosophies than the ones we had become used to when we were at Rover. It was a mind broadening experience for all of us.

We had set ourselves a slogan at the start-up of the company based on the statement that we were reasonably unique as we came from senior levels of the automobile industry and its design departments. We had a good inside knowledge of how a large company worked from a senior level. We also had an interesting insight into the approach of in-house design studios to companies like us. When working in those in-house studios ourselves we knew what was important to us and by becoming consultants ourselves, we knew the pitfalls there were, we knew what aspects of the relationships had not appealed to us as in-house designers, and what to do as independent consultants, to increase the respect between consultancies and design departments.

We liked to bring that point along when talking to new customers, plus we had the basic slogan of saying we would 'complete the work on time to an agreed price and to expectations'. If the time allowed for the project was exceeded or the work required was exceeded, as long as it was not as a result of changes to the terms and references as originally laid out, we would meet the price we quoted at the beginning and would absorb the extra cost if we got it wrong.

This was stressed because when I was in the big companies and receiving work from outside consultancies from time to time, overruns were a frequent difficulty. What often happened was that in order to get the business, these consultancies would put in a low bid, miscalculate the actual amount of work required to complete the job and then when they were three quarters of the way through they would descend upon us and demand more money and with a project so far along they usually got it.

We felt bad about the consultancies that did that, and in some cases the situation was bad enough never to go back to them again. One of the points we wanted to make to prospective customers to DRAL was that this would not happen, as we would always stick to our quote, even if we miscalculated and lost money ourselves. This led to us rarely putting in a rock bottom bid; that would happen only if we were going to try and break into some new area of business and were prepared to take the risk.

Generally speaking our bids were considered high by our customers, but we also had a very high incidence of repeat business, which indicated to us that although our prices were upscale, so was the satisfaction level we were aiming for in our quotation. We were on time and on price subject to no direction changes by the client and our third leg was to say that we would complete the work at least to our customer's satisfaction, but we always aimed to exceed that and usually did.

Work on cars was not always for the large companies; we worked on a number of projects, most notably an idea that was developed in the early 1990s by Jim Randle. The ex-Jaguar engineering director was keen on hybrid cars when no one else knew about them and he particularly latched on to the idea applied to a taxi.

This seemed to us to be a very good idea indeed, because the hybrid is best in city situations. Whereas on long fast journeys there's little to be gained, a taxi usually operates in urban areas, so was the ideal application. Jim was working with the British

Taxi project looked promising and delivered a frustrating result

taxi company, LTI, to develop this idea, and we worked with him at his invitation to see how this vehicle would look. We extended this to show how the interior would look, and how it could be redesigned to give added safety to the driver.

This design was taken quite a long way, in fact, we used the exterior model for a project as one of our studio entrance foyer exhibits and it always created considerable interest. We financed most of the early work on the body design over Jim's chassis layouts, but the project did not fly in the end, and much to our great annoyance another thing happened, which one has to be careful of in the design consultancy business.

This was that the taxi manufacturer used another designer who had been influenced by our project's shapes and forms and adopted our design theme and general appearance. That vehicle was produced without the hybrid drivetrain, but had a distinct visual likeness to ours. You can certainly threaten a lawsuit or something of the sort for misuse of the design, but usually at the end of the day, the expense is not worth the trip. Unfortunately, on that occasion, we had to grin and bear it.

Our relationship with Rolls-Royce was always very good in this respect, because the designs produced were jointly registered as designs for Rolls-Royce and we were paid for that. Therefore, it was a legal situation and we had no claim against them, or they against us, and I think RR was very sensible in that regard.

With most companies we just simply took that risk when working on prototypes. So, say we did a job for Honda, produced a full-sized model and then sent it to them, they would pay their bill and that would be that. We would accept that if they used the design, then we could not go back saying we demand a royalty because that was not the way we entered into the agreement with them. Honda, of course is a very honourable company, which creates a strong trust between the parties.

The work doing those prototypes was very satisfying, we always had good relationships with the 'in house' designers, in many cases people we knew well, we had good sit down discussions and produced a comprehensive analysis of how we thought their company was viewed by the outside world.

This was a better service than those where consultants had been coming to us in the past, as we rarely heard of our consultants' views as to the company they were engaged by. We were rather keen to present that to our customers and it was always a key component in our presentation of our projects.

Our customers always received this considered view of the project extremely well and we developed a format of producing a book, which we would then present to the customer at the time of the design completion. This gave our analysis of our way of thinking, and of reaching a conclusion as why the design we were presenting was appropriate for them in our view. This book took the reader through a research, sketch, and final model builds phase. It was an impressive little book to give each of our customers at that time of the final presentation of our work to them.

On our first meeting with RR, we were asked by Peter Ward and Mike Donovan to formulate our thoughts for a new larger Bentley to replace the Mulsanne. We did a very thorough, internally generated analysis on this project, and came up with our image of how Rolls-Royce would have continued if the change of direction after the S2 design had not taken place. By that I mean going on from the Silver Cloud before things got a little lost.

After early 2D work had been well received, we put together a full-sized clay model with the involvement of Graham Hull, who was Rolls-Royce's in-house designer, to illustrate how this would look and the reception of the model by Peter and Mike was very encouraging. Peter and the Rolls-Royce team liked what they saw, and understood what we were trying to say, and at this point the clay model was turned over to them to turn into a reality by RR engineering. The design was copyrighted jointly between RR and us and was, in due course, produced as the Bentley Arnage.

It's interesting when you look at that car alongside the Bentley GT and the new Rolls-Royce Phantom, that there seems to be more tradition and presence in the Arnage. Though, as I write, it is being replaced as a ten years old design. Though I have not seen the new model in the flesh I am pleased with the look in such pictures as I have seen so far. The company is now a part of VW, of course and the design is in house but it looks right to me. In contrast the latest Rolls-Royce cars, the company now owned by BMW and also designed in house, specifically the Phantom to my eyes is very much overstated, even ugly, to my eyes gross is the American word! The new smaller Ghost, also not seen in the flesh, is better but oh that grille, it has none of the majesty of the original which was so carefully protected over the years, what a waste. When we worked with RR/Bentley, the grille was an all-important thing to protect. To today's buyers, this may not be too important, but I do feel that it still is. As the grille form gets more and more distorted, then the uniqueness of the brand becomes more and more diluted. Take off the badge of a Bentley GT and Flying Spur, and if you did not know, it would not immediately say 'Bentley'. Time will tell.

I think, from that point of view people who were buying Rolls-Royces and looking for traditionally British products, our design had those qualities. The Arnage would appeal to people who liked understated dignity. I think the design direction of the new Rolls-Royce has qualities suited more to a military vehicle than a large luxury saloon. The whole thing comes across as very unpleasant, it's brutal, large and in your face but I guess it has an appeal to some people.

Bentley Java was designed by DRA and predicted the company's move to sportier, more compact cars

The Bentley marque under VW went the other way. The GT looks good, but the Flying Spur as a four-door car is rather anonymous, though beautifully made and finished, with an interior similar to the one we did for the Java.

I think it's interesting to see how the two companies have split apart under BMW and Volkswagen, but sadly neither has gone in the direction I would have liked to see them go, though I admit that they have had success with what they have done.

It became something of a tradition at DRAL to produce a scale model of something that would be of interest to us, and to use that model to be a focus in our foyer. It proved to be a good tactic, and these models influenced many visiting companies favourably.

I was looking for something in 1993/4 to replace a large yacht model we had on show at the time. My own car was a Mercedes-Benz SL500, and I always had felt that a car in this category would be right, such as a Bentley.

As confidentiality is a delicate subject in the consultancy business, I decided to ask permission from Peter Ward, who we were developing a good relationship with at this time, to do a model of this idea for our own use in this way, and his response was more than I expected.

He said that they had been considering a smaller Bentley idea themselves, as the world economies were in a market downturn, and RR was really struggling with a range of only very large expensive cars. Peter felt that there was a case for a smaller Bentley, but it was very hard to judge what the reaction would be by the traditional buyers of full-size premium cars, basically he didn't want to shoot himself in the foot! After discussion, we agreed that it would be of real interest to investigate the idea, but in full size and with the requirement that the design should be a four-seater.

RR did not have the money to finance this, but I decided that it was worth proposing a joint venture, with us producing a full size proposal at half our normal fee, and with RR paying the other half, only if the model proved to be something they wanted to pursue from there.

We produced the model with Graham Hull, the RR designer at the time, being involved, and with certain restrictions being laid down. The size was roughly that of a 5-Series BMW, and it was essential to carry over the Bentley grille theme, though some latitude on proportion was allowed in the end. The result created considerable excitement at RR, and the project went ahead with the production of a full-size fibreglass model, which RR decided to show at the Geneva show in 1994.

Another bit of good news was that our full fee was paid with this decision!

There was, however, still a degree of nervousness at RR, and they proposed to me that if they showed the car at Geneva, they wanted to show it as a concept exercise supported by RR. But they wanted to keep a distance between us officially, so we would be identified as a consultant who had been engaged to look at this idea.

This we agreed to, as it gave us a wonderful exercise in free publicity. In the event, close to the last minute, RR changed tactic. They really liked the finished design and wanted to present it as their own, with DRAL being the design house that produced it. We agreed, and the model was shown to great acclaim, with ourselves to the forefront at the launch. Altogether a very satisfying exercise and with a great result for us too.

This model was shown worldwide as a concept for a future smaller Bentley, and proved to be a very credible thing in most people's eyes. Only the shortage of funds prevented a smaller Bentley from seeing the light of day. This was one more of those lost opportunities by the British owned car company.

I have to say that the time we set up and ran DRAL was the most interesting part of my career. This nine-year final stage of my career has been satisfying because it provided the opportunity to work with so many different clients at the same time. There was a considerable amount of very interesting work, and also the opportunity to learn from a master like Les Wharton how to run a business and keep it afloat.

I say that with some feeling because soon after we became independent and got going, we had a lesson in the difficulties that can arise with such operations. We had a contract that did not get fulfilled, and we found ourselves in some unexpected difficulties. We got out of it, but it was a salutary lesson on how business goes if you're a small and independent operation, there isn't very much of a safety net around so it did teach us something very important. This is a very different thing to running a department in a large company.

However, the rest of the time was very successful, and we had a considerable range of projects to do and some very interesting clients as well, altogether a very satisfying experience and conclusion to my career.

We were able to conduct our business debt free for the life of the company. Unfortunately one of the difficulties of running a company like this as I have related earlier is that much of the work done is under the strict rules of confidentiality. Therefore even in a book like this, well after the event, it would be very unethical of me to disclose many of the things we did. Projects were done with clients who, in many cases, had their own design departments, we had insights into what they were doing, we had opportunities for inputting into their programmes, and I feel that I need to be very careful in not betraying any trusts.

The matter of confidentiality was difficult with respect to keeping our company visible. I had many contacts in the automotive press and we engaged Geoff Courtney, who I had known in his journalistic days and his time with Aston Martin.

Geoff became our consultant on these matters, but it was a very difficult task, as there was always so much we could not discuss with the press. We did produce some excellent brochures, and Geoff arranged many interviews with journalists with a number of good articles about us being written and published.

There are a few examples of the products we were involved in that can be talked about; our relationship with Rolls-Royce had flourished in the early days and we got involved in a project for one very special customer, who shall remain nameless, but who was active in the speciality car market at this time. We were able therefore to put together some quite spectacular projects all based on Bentley cars and the work was extremely varied, most unusual and quite unique. It was like going back in time when the coachbuilding industry was alive and well and producing unique deigns for wealthy customers.

Around 1998, I was feeling that I should be looking for an exit strategy leading to retirement. I had been handing more responsibility to Adrian Griffiths and Graham Lewis, but this was not the way to continue the business, even though I had hoped it would be.

We began talking to a number of companies that had been consultants to us at Rover and DRAL. This was not a sudden decision, it evolved through working together over a period of time. One company that we talked to was MGA, the company we had been involved with making many show quality fibreglass models for us to our designs including the Java for RR, and we'd been very pleased with the work they'd done for us over a period of time.

It became an almost natural thing to start talking about gaining something through potentially merging our companies to mutual advantage. I had some longstanding feelings about design companies, particularly how they operated worldwide. There were a lot of people producing product design of one kind or another and those companies that were successful over the long term were often very firmly design (style) led.

Their designers were people who attracted potential customers to place work with them, but engineering was often the company goal and money-maker, and the company's leaders were engineers who understood that business better.

The way the Italian design houses had set up their operations, was that they were creative design houses, and had the advantage of being perceived by just about everyone as people with style and the place to go to get it. They later developed engineering and in some cases production capability but style remained as the thing they were selling and were famous for.

The Italians were unique with their work. There were similarities to the French who, in the 1930s, would produce knockout designs in terms of new ideas, themes and thoughts yet the volume car industry was littered with rather sad design solutions. Italian production cars, with some notable exceptions, were not known for their beauty, particularly Fiat and even Alfa Romeo post-war, they never seemed to hit the target with their four-door saloons.

The Italian coachbuilding industry thrived on the production of wonderful and inspirational ideas. An example of one design house which flourished from pre to post-war was Superleggera Touring. You look at the influential Barchetta Ferrari that was produced just after the war, to see this was where their skills carried through.

However along with Bertone, Pininfarina and the newcomers Ital Design, the Italian design houses have managed to survive and flourish, and the make up of these companies was very much design led. By this I mean that the designer name was the attraction for the customer, and this provided the inspiration for them. The world is changing, and it is becoming very hard to make any design consultancy work profitably. Most big global companies now have at least one off-base advanced studio feeding ideas into the main company studio, reducing the need for independent design house input.

I felt this type of operation was something the British could really emulate, but they could never get around the problem of engineering vs design. I guess my major regret during my career was that I didn't establish a company that was truly design led a lot earlier in my career.

Maybe that was too ambitious a thing to do in the climate of that time, but it was something I would have loved to try. It was something the French and the Americans couldn't do either, just the Italians, who had the right image.

It was achievable, but it would have taken a long time to establish, and only with the right kind of backing. It would have been extremely satisfying to do that, but it was not to be.

After numerous discussions with many people about how we could move the company along, a company which was looking for some specific work approached us. This company, Ove Arup Associates, is a global architectural engineering consultancy. It is large with an automotive division providing specialised engineering automotive help of a technical nature.

Over a short period, it was agreed with John Miles of Ove Arup, that there was a similarity in the goals of the two companies that could lead to more collaboration. These discussions eventually came to fruition, and we were able to sell the company to Ove Arup in order to continue, I hoped, along the lines DRAL had done before and that Arup would take it on from there.

The whole industry was in transition, and we were moving from basically artist's work, to a more computer-oriented approach to design. I don't believe front-end creative design should be one hundred per cent computer produced, but obviously this transition was going ahead and still is.

Arup had a lot of knowledge in this area, so I felt that would project the thing forward. In fact after I retired, Arup did try to set up a design led operation, but I do not feel that the engineers really grasped what I was talking about, and in fact, when I said 'design led operation', I think they thought I meant 'design engineering operation'.

It just seemed impossible for those engineers to grasp that fundamental thing, and the thought of them working in some kind of subservient way to the aesthetic designer was just not acceptable. As a result, that idea did not fly. These are personal views, of course.

The company shrunk under Arup, and to be fair this was also due to big changes in the industry, which made life much more difficult for consultancies and many of those we had talked to earlier had gone out of business altogether. I am glad to say that a smaller 'DRAL' is still in existence today under the ARUP name.

It is now operating in a different way. No longer do they have the premises we had or the model making ability, it has evolved into something else. That's the way things have to be I guess.

Looking back at over 40 years in the design business, I have no regrets at all. Most of my career was at design director level, which gave me a wonderful overview of the business. I count myself so fortunate for being one of those people who knew what they wanted to be when they were as young as six, seven or eight years old, and I was one of those people who managed to achieve that result by good fortune and being in the right place at the right time. I have been able to follow that path all of my life and I could not have asked for more.

I ended up retiring, feeling, from the point of view of my working life, that I was extremely satisfied with the experience I have had. Through that period I was strongly supported by my wonderful wife of 49 years, and I have two great children who have done well in their lives, and we have eight wonderful grandchildren.

My son Chris is a car designer too, so that is also very satisfying, and I'm intrigued to see my youngest grandson who's still only five having this fascination with things with wheels and with drawing. I just wonder if he'll develop in that way as well, we shall find out in the fullness of time.

One final word is a tribute to the secretaries who put up with me for many years. When your job is one of almost constant travel, and with a very busy schedule it is essential to have a good secretary or office administrator, as they are sometimes called, with a good knowledge of the business of design. In the UK before my transfer to Chrysler in Detroit, we did not have a real secretary until the Chrysler UK and Europe days, but then it became a very necessary thing.

When I moved to Detroit I inherited, so to speak, Colin Neal's secretary, Betty, who had been with him for all his time at Chrysler. I was not sure how it would work out as she was fiercely devoted to Colin and very protective. When I first visited Chrysler in the late 1960s, she was almost a formidable figure. All was well, however and Betty transferred this loyalty to me though the protection was sometimes more than I wanted, I like to have an 'open door'!

After I was promoted to wider responsibilities at Chrysler, Marlene Lynn became my secretary. Marlene was a gracious and a highly competent secretary, and a good friend. We always exchange Christmas cards and up to date news. She eventually, much later, became Tom Gale's secretary, when he was on the Board at DaimlerChrysler, and I did get to see her again on occasional visits I made to Chrysler during the 1990s.

At ARG, I had a similar situation strangely enough. I inherited David Bache's secretary Maureen Hill. Maureen had been with David since from the first time she had a job I believe and she also was very loyal to David. In the circumstances I expected a problem, but again it did not materialise, Maureen transferred her loyalty to me, and proved to be very competent. So much so, that I eventually promoted Maureen to run the office administration, a position that she eventually retired from. She, also is a good friend who I keep in touch with.

When at DRAL, my administration assistant was Pam Cox who ran things very well in a very different situation to that in the big companies.

All these ladies did an invaluable job; it would have been chaos without them.

Over the years I have travelled many more miles than I ever expected. This was a experience on many occasions too when aircraft failed or left me stranded in some remote location. I have had the pleasure of travelling in proximity to many of the rich and famous. I well remember a journey from Japan to the UK stopping as it did in those days in Anchorage to refuel. On this occasion the plane failed in some way, and we had to stay overnight. Peter Ustinov was a fellow passenger and he entertained the first class passengers over dinner in a most hilarious way. It came as a disappointment when the plane was fixed!

I also had a pleasant journey across the USA to Los Angeles sitting next to Ernest Borgnine, who turned out to be a most agreeable companion. I was also on a similar trip with Sean Connery sitting across the aisle. There were many other such occasions and also many scary experiences too. There were many strange destinations such as a visit to a bus plant in Roswell New Mexico, where the great spacecraft landing was supposed to have taken place just after the war. After my visit I understood why they never came back!

21

Thoughts from Retirement

I HAVE FREQUENTLY BEEN ASKED why I always seemed to work for companies that were not the 'most glamorous'. It is true that I have spent a great deal of my career building up new or revitalised design operations in companies that have had a stormy background. I have no regrets. The earliest days were an opportunity to help establish design in the industry in Europe. This was tough and often hard going but stimulating too.

The chance to plan and expand the operations and take a more responsible role was very satisfying and I was lucky to have opportunities come my way to further the cause.

The work I was responsible for was in the volume end of the market, but in the final ten years before retirement, it encompassed both the volume and the high end of the market. In my opinion, to design a one-model low volume supercar or a show car or 'one off' is a much easier task than the design task involved in a high volume vehicle but the exposure to the press is much greater with the former.

No problem there, but it perhaps explains why there can be so much satisfaction in working in the volume environment. The MG EX-E and the Rover CCV were designs that received a great deal of publicity, but they were relatively easy to do with relatively minimal feasibility requirements. The same applied later when consulting for other companies where creative ideas were at a premium, but where total feasibility for production had to be done by the in-house team of the company we were working for. The balance of this range of projects gave me considerable satisfaction over the years.

At the end of WW2, the motor industry was an exciting place to be. New models were introduced between 1945 and 1950 that were a big move forward from the pre-war offerings. America provided the inspiration both by their new 'styled' cars, dramatically changing the scene, and also the fact that Britain and the rest of Europe had to export to pull out of the disaster of wartime, and the only place in the world that could afford cars for the general population, was the USA. These cars had to appeal to a new kind of market and new model development was going on at a fast pace in the UK.

Looking at the industry today, it is in a sorry state. There has been much merging of companies, most of which has been very misguided. I think that in my career in the industry I have not seen one of these 'Chairman's ego' mergers work, with the possible exception of Renault/Nissan. Not only that but instead of the weaker companies falling by the wayside they have been 'saved' by such mergers only to contribute more and more to the overcapacity in the industry.

The great world recession of 2008 has produced some startling scenarios. The USA domestic manufacturers are crippled and may not all survive particularly, I feel, as government has become involved! My experiences in a government owned car industry in UK taught me that the combination of politicians and industry is caustic and just does not work. Time will tell but I have great forebodings as to the eventual fate of the domestic USA car industry. The Japanese and also the Koreans are moving ahead and VW is a rising force too with Mercedes, BMW and Lexus being the undisputed leaders in the luxury market segment. There is still a great deal of over capacity in the industry which has shown no real appetite for culling dead brands unless forced to do so but perhaps that time has come and will be of benefit to the industry as a whole.

Against this scenario, the technology and competence of manufacture in the industry has made huge strides. I, and others, predicted 30 years ago that cars would be so competent in their engineering in the future, that quality and reliability would be a given and that choice of purchase would be by price, practicality for purpose and the look of the product.

This has been true for the development of most consumer products in the period and has resulted in many fine products today. The quality and reliability of these products has a downside to manufacturers, as they are longer lasting, but the appearance and feature content updates tend to balance this, tempting buyers to change more frequently.

Car design has come a long way but today's product tends to be overweighed by features and impractical performance capabilities, many of which are gimmicks, which results in too much energy consumption and a nightmare to service. The enormous weight added by today's safety features alone is very energy consuming, and sometimes with doubtful effectiveness.

The whole thing is now very political due to oil being the only real practical propellant at this time. Unwisely, the USA, the major user to date, decided in the past, rather than use their own reserves, to use up cheap oil from counties that have not exactly used the proceeds to the benefit of everyone.

Now the resistance to allow new drilling in the USA is causing a crisis. New technology is a way away, however, and all forms of energy need to be developed to get out of this problem, and much time and money will be wasted in this quest. Bigger vehicles have been rightly criticised, but this is valid only because of their greater energy consumption. Hybrids sell because they can offer size at the same consumption of oil as a smaller car (not totally true), but the cost and complexity, which also consumes energy but elsewhere, is considerable. A forced political solution is not the way I fear. A great deal of taxpayers' money is about to be wasted on dead ends. Right now, diesel fuel offers a great opportunity, which Europe has embraced, but which the USA has viewed with blinkers on.

Design is now big business. When I first joined the Rootes studios, there were six of us. Now design departments of major companies run to hundreds. The products are competent and exciting, but there is a real loss of individuality, which is largely caused by the risk involved in designing a product some four to five years ahead of production, and hitting the acceptance envelope of the customer at the time of introduction.

The lack of real individuality in the mainstream product today, levels the playing field, but misses out on the opportunity to break out from the herd. Designers have a tough job today, but so did we in the past when we were fighting for the chance to have our ideas break through the resistance of the established engineering and manufacturing positions. The scenario today is much more integrated, and the results are very well resolved as a result.

I am as enthusiastic about car design as ever. It has been a great pleasure to be part of the business when so much has happened. I have also met so many talented people, made many friends, and hopefully have been able to help a significant number of young people achieve their dreams too.

I hope to retain that enthusiasm for a few years yet, and perhaps the next few years will bring about some really exciting and revolutionary new developments

Lightning Source UK Ltd.
Milton Keynes UK
29 November 2010

163612UK00006B/31/P